This Belongs To:

D1595665

MANN AT SEA

Derek Mann

VANTAGE PRESS
New York

FIRST EDITION

Published by Vantage Press, Inc.
516 West 34th Street, New York, New York 10001

Manufactured in the United States of America
ISBN: 0-533-10952-3

Library of Congress Catalog Card No.: 93-95065

0 9 8 7 6 5 4 3 2 1

To Barbara, my wife and shipmate. Her enthusiasm and caring make life happy and exciting for all who sail the seven seas with her.

Contents

Foreword

For much of the 1980s, my wife, Mary, and I sailed as lecturers and occasionally host and hostess on board all three original Royal Viking ships. Our favorite was always *Royal Viking Star;* I am sure that one reason we so enjoyed her was that Derek and Barbara Mann served as cruise director and hostess. We first met them on a press cruise to Barbados back in 1981 and sailed with them many times over the years that followed.

Derek had a cheerful and accessible office amidships, looking out onto the promenade deck. Each day, he posted in his window a ribald cartoon or mock pronouncement that passengers enjoyed as they trudged past. Additionally, I recall with especial pleasure the evening entertainments Derek mounted, long before prerecorded production shows took over. They were in the finest tradition of inventive, theatrical fun. One hilarious performance stays with me still: Derek, clad in a yellow tutu and wrinkled tights, brandishing an ineffectual magic wand and convulsing the entire passenger load with a bravura number.

But patently, there is more to Derek Mann than fun and games. He is a fine raconteur and when he told me he had written a cruising memoir, I suggested I read it and, if I liked it, write this foreword. Well, I did and I have.

To my mind, *Mann at Sea* is invaluable on two counts—first, as an extremely useful guide for passengers sailing anywhere on any vessel; second, as an opportunity to share cruise director Derek's unique vantage point, offering behind-the-scenes glimpses of life on board a luxurious passenger vessel. He has assembled a glorious cast—impossible passengers, famous passengers, passengers who miss the boat, passengers who die at sea, captains, crises, storms, alarms, and, always, laughter. Derek's shipboard is a rich mélange, uncommonly well told.

I have always felt that concealed beneath the alphabetized names of a passenger list or hidden behind rows of anonymous portholes lurked a wealth of compelling drama. My hat goes off to Derek Mann for bringing so much of that drama to life in these entertaining pages. This is mandatory reading for passengers, crew, shore staff, and, without question, marine historians.

—John Maxtone-Graham
New York, Spring 1994

Acknowledgments

I wish to thank Mrs. Marian McLeland, an editor of note, who first suggested this book and donated her time and skill in making my first manuscript readable. My thanks also go to Gary Oakes, Lou Garcia, and Carmen and Andreas Torres (Los Malagas). These four talented artists, producers, and choreographers have created such wonderful shows for me over the years. In those shows have been so many talented performers. You are far too numerous to be mentioned by name, but you all know who you are. My heartfelt thanks to all of you.

Introduction

I appreciate that many of you might never have cruised before. Therefore, in writing this book, my purpose was to share with you life on board a cruise ship.

Part I of the book acquaints you with ship life and tells you not only about the duties and responsibilities of the officers' crew and those of a Cruise Director but about many of the things you should know to enable you to enjoy what is the best vacation of all: a cruise. There are, in addition, vignettes that are incidental to this information.

Part II acquaints you with the background of your humble author: the introduction to my first voyage and my first love as well as the impetus for my becoming the genial guide and Master of Ceremonies I am today for those ready to savor life at sea.

Part III contains those stories collected during my years as a Cruise Director on many ships and many cruises.

And last, Part IV comprises cruising tips that, I hope, will assist you in the preparation and organization of a cruise itself.

At this point, you may well ask, "What does a Cruise Director do?" Primarily, the job is to keep the passengers happy and occupied. A Cruise Director schedules and creates the Daily Program and acts as Master of Ceremonies at the various shows. Cruise Directors like me, who are performers, are expected to do at least one major show a cruise. We are required to lecture expertly on all ports of call, and we must have knowledge of local currency, taxi rates, and, more important, of where the restroooms are at each stop.

For many years I worked for Royal Viking Line (the "Cadillac" of cruise lines), a world cruise line that enjoyed many days at sea. My day's agenda might include as many as sixty different activities. On long cruises, my staff might number up to fifty people. In arranging for Enrichment Lectures and special guests, I was involved with every level of society: They could be royalty, ambassadors, presidents, high ranking government and CIA officials, as well as film stars and television personalities. The evenings would often involve three or four cocktail parties and as many shows. It was a wonderfully busy and glamorous life.

Since leaving Royal Viking in 1987, I have worked as a consultant or Cruise Director for four other major cruise lines. For the last six years, I have been working as Cruise Director for Regency Cruises. This company, inaugurated in 1986, has six ships, offering cruises accessible to vacationers in all walks of life. Creating new programs for their ever-expanding horizons has been a challenging, gratifying experience.

I hope the reader will enjoy the stories about persons, places, and adventures, all of which are true (though, in many cases, I am not able to use the real names of those personalities who have enriched my life). I know my cruising companions always eagerly await that moment when, after dinner at the Cruise Director's table, coffee is served and the stories begin.

MANN AT SEA

I

A Floating Hotel

Cruising used to be considered strictly the domain of the wealthy. That is no longer the case. The seas of the world are now a playground for all. With so many cruise ships, fares have become very competitive. You can cruise for as little as $120 or as much as $1,000 a day. This includes food and entertainment. Cruising gives you a lot for your money. Literally millions of Americans have not yet had the thrill of sailing on a cruise ship. Research shows that only 6 percent of the American public have cruised. What is it about cruising that makes it so different from other vacations? Sean Meaney, a well-known cruise director, when asked what he thought about cruising, replied, "Well, take away the ship, and what do you have?"

The fact is that you would be experiencing just another luxury hotel if the ship were not at sea. But a ship moves; it has form and a language all its own. It has a port side and a starboard side, a prow and a stern. The engine room is its heart, and the bridge its brain. A ship becomes a demanding mistress for those who care for her. She, sexist reference though it may be, needs constant attention: fueling, cleaning, painting, repairing. The officers and crew usually leave their loved ones and families at home to care for her. A floating hotel has unique problems—different from those one would expect. You cannot go down the road and buy a replacement part when you are hundreds of miles out at sea. Living on board is very confining, and you cannot walk too far away from problems. They must be faced and dealt with right there and then. Officers and crew have to be very conscious of safety codes, rules, and regulations. It is a disciplined living in a civilian environment, and not everyone finds it that easy to deal with. Cooperation and teamwork between all departments are of utmost importance, creating an atmosphere for a happy crew. A happy crew makes for happy passengers. The image of a cruise is one of quality living. Service and cleanliness are essential. Those who work on board have to love the sea and really care for their job. The dedication shown by the ship's personnel, especially in senior management, gives cruising that edge over other vacation options. Yes, it's the ship that makes the difference, and the crew who makes the place.

A ship is comprised of three departments: deck, engine, and hotel. The hotel is the largest by virtue of the number of pursers, cruise staff, entertainers, waiters, stewards, stewardesses, and cleaners.

The hotel is headed by the hotel manager, who supervises the department heads, including the chief purser, the cruise director, the chief steward or food manager, the housekeeper, and the bar manager. The food manager's department heads are the chef and the maître d'.

The chief engineer heads the Engine Department and is responsible for every working part on the ship. The department heads are the assistant chief engineer (whose main working area is the engine room), the chief electrician, and the refrigeration or air-conditioning engineer.

The Deck Department is headed by the deputy or staff captain, who, on behalf of the captain, has the chief radio officer, the chief officer, the navigator, the safety officer, and the doctor as department heads. As for overall command of the ship, the captain's decision is final in all matters. His word is law, as the expression goes, and the captain bears full responsibility for all matters arising on board. In my early days of cruising, there was a show of respect accorded the captain by both crew and passengers. One stood when the captain came into the room, spoke to you, or came to your table. These days, although the captain still gets respect, it is rarely shown in a formal manner. However, I still train my staff to do so.

Different shipping companies have different ways of dealing with their officers, staff, and crew. For senior management, the contract time averages around four months. Basically, you are on duty twenty-four hours a day. A working day, without unforeseen circumstances, lasts about fourteen hours. On land, a forty-hour week is the norm. In four months, that works out to 640 hours, not counting holidays. Landlubbers go home at five. They don't have to socialize with the people they work with, and they have weekends off. The total number of work hours for the same period at sea in many cases is 1,568, nearly one year's work in four months. It is not always the easy, glamorous job it appears to be.

The cruise director heads the Cruise Department, answering directly to the hotel manager and, on some ships, to the captain. The assistant helps run the day-to-day operation and schedules the staff for the events created by the cruise director. Some assistants also produce the daily program on a computer before it goes to the printer. All ships have a print shop, some more sophisticated than others. On the Royal Viking Line, the operation not only included a printer but a professional editor. The shop itself had a proper offset printing press and could print the newspaper in color if required. Most ships publish a broadsheet program of daily events and information. This is produced by the cruise director, who collects information from various departments. When the master is finished, it is sent to the printer, who runs off the program for distribution to the passengers.

The social director is responsible for bringing people together in as many ways as possible. I have been fortunate to have my wife as my social director or hostess. Barbara first greeted me on the gangway of the *Royal Viking Sea* in 1975. We married in 1980 in the chapel of the *Royal Viking Star*. Barbara is considered one of the best in the industry. She is successful because she cares for people and works hard to keep them happy and occupied. Besides being gregarious, a hostess must be a good listener and be calm in a time of crisis. Making friends and meeting people are what cruising and being a hostess are all about.

The Shore Excursion Department usually comes under the Cruise Department. The shore excursion manager deals with selling tours, land operators, and general shoreside dispatch, which entails getting passengers smoothly off the ship and efficiently organizing their departure onto the buses. The job calls for a great deal of knowledge of ports and tours being offered. Tour managers have to be patient, understanding, and imperturbable. It is not an easy job. Buses break down, transport fails to arrive on time, bad weather— all add up to the many frustrations in the life of a shore excursion manager.

The Cruise Department includes many talented people. Most ships have a production team, consisting of perhaps six young dancers and singers. This group performs a minimum of two shows on a seven-day cruise and often operates as cruise staff during the day. Other artists can include a musical act, a magician, a juggler, or a comedian. The daytime program requires other than the normal cruise staff to keep you happy. You will have enrichment lectures by experts who will speak on a host of subjects that, it is hoped, will be of interest to you. These subjects can be anything from oceanography to money to history, or possibly a celebrity may talk about his or her career or life. Many ships provide bridge directors and arts and crafts or dance instructors. For cruises over seven days, most companies have on board a clergyman, representing one of the major faiths.

The dance host program has become popular and is often included now on many ships. Gentlemen who are gregarious and who enjoy dancing are employed to see to it that social life is enhanced, especially for the single ladies. At the time this book was written, more and more cruise lines were staffing their ships with hosts, even for the short seven-day cruises. Many single women, especially, shall we say, the more mature in years, are reluctant to cruise. However, I can assure those with doubts about a cruise vacation that it is probably the best form of holiday for the single lady. Maître d's are always very helpful in their table planning to ensure that single gentlemen, if available, are seated with single ladies. A singles party is held to get them acquainted with each other and with the staff.

Then there is the fact of being safe on a ship. One charming story comes to mind regarding a single lady who needed escorting in a way not usually associated with a cruise ship. During a sixty-seven-day Circle Pacific cruise, a lady phoned the Purser's Office and asked for a taxi to take her to the dining room. The Purser's Office asked me what they should do. The lady, a Miss Francis, would not accept that there were no cabs on the ship. I called her and told her a cab would be along in a few minutes. I went to her cabin, knocked on the door, and told her that her cab was waiting.

The door was opened by a very well-dressed lady in her sixties. I said, "Good evening," and offered my arm, which she took. As we walked to the dining room, we had a nice chat about the ship and the weather. I escorted her to the maître d' and told him that Miss Francis would like a cab after dinner to drive her either to the theater, the show lounge, or to her cabin. I explained that my cab company would make sure she was brought to the dining room every evening about this time.

From then on, for the next sixty-five days, I or one of my

staff would pick up Miss Francis. She never required "transportation" for breakfast or lunch. She received no bill from our Gold Cab Company, as we became known. However, on her comment sheet, devoid of any other comment, she wrote: "This ship has the most pleasant cab drivers I have ever met." And I always thought I was in the cruise business.

Health and exercise have become very prominent in the daily program, so you will find an energetic fitness director to keep you slim and healthy. A cruise-ship program that revolves around food needs a good exercise program to keep the weight down. Because of all the food you will be enjoying, it is important that you have as much exercise as possible whilst on the ship. By exercise, I don't necessarily mean leaping about in the gym or in the aerobics classes. A good, long walk is also a way of keeping fit. Contrary to what you might have been told, it is not the salt in the air that shrinks your clothes.

By now, you have some idea of the officers, staff, and crew on board a cruise ship. Let us now imagine you are going to take your first cruise. You have been to your travel agent and decided on a cruise to some sunny clime. The ports you wish to visit, and the ship that suits your taste and pocket have been chosen. You are probably excited and wish to invite friends to see you off. Security is very tight on ships since the hijacking of the *Achille Lauro*. If you wish to invite guests to your bon voyage party, you will have to apply for passes well before sailing day. Your travel agent will advise you on the procedure.

The shipping line brochure has given you an idea of what the social life is like on board. Let us assume you have chosen a ship that has a dress code other than jeans and a swimsuit. You can look forward to two formal nights a week; this would require a black tie or a suit for the gentlemen and a long or a cocktail dress for the ladies. Two other nights may be semiformal or informal. These would entail a jacket and tie (with trousers) for the gentlemen and a dress or pantsuit for the ladies. Day clothing is casual as it is for the other evenings when advertised. I would then suggest that casual be casually smart or elegant. It is not acceptable to wear shorts or cutaway jeans after 6:00 P.M.! On formal evenings, neither is it proper to change into casual wear after dinner. That's fine for the cinema or on deck, but not for public lounges or the showroom. Elegance and good taste have always been very much a part of cruising, and, on the few times that the dress code suggests formal, it is a shame to destroy the atmosphere of a gala evening.

Let's suppose those last moments have arrived when you are ready to leave your home. Given my experience of listening to passengers' tales of woe, I can remind you of one or two last-minute things you might forget to do. Make sure you have all of your tickets, your passport, and your money. Do *not* put any of this into a bag! If at all possible, put them all into a pocket right on your person. Remember to take your camera and your binoculars, if you own a pair. When you finish packing your bags, make sure you have two labels securely attached to each one: one should be the shipping-line label with the port of embarkation, cabin number, etc.; the other label should be on your bag all the time, with your name, address, and telephone number clearly shown. With so many bags looking alike, it is very easy to pick up the wrong one. Barbara festoons our suitcases with colored ribbons; so if anybody did walk off with ours by mistake, he or she would have to be blind or just plain barmy. Having done all that, make sure you have closed all windows, locked all doors, and provided for the cat. Lastly, take the house keys with you to get back in.

Congratulations! You have at last arrived at your port of disembarkation to which many of you had to fly. It is hoped that representatives of the shipping line will be at the port to greet you. After you have collected your baggage, they will organize your transportation to the ship. If the baggage has been mislaid by the airline, you will have to fill out a form, describing the details of the lost bags. The ship's agents and representatives will endeavor to get them to the ship, either before the ship sails or at the next port. If there is a real problem in finding lost baggage, the airline will okay you to buy clothes up to a certain figure (I mean money, not shape). One last comment on lost baggage: The staff and crew will always do their best to lend you some clothes, especially for that first formal evening. It can be embarrassing for a fine couple to meet the captain if the wife appears in a creased pantsuit and the husband looks as if he has just washed the car.

The most horrendous luggage story I remember was an incident that occurred in Los Angeles at the start of a sixty-seven-day Circle Pacific cruise. Booked into one of the main suites for the complete voyage was a VIP couple. When they arrived at Los Angeles airport, two of their ten pieces of luggage were missing. These two pieces contained all of the wife's exclusive formal evening gowns, recently purchased in Paris and New York.

The ship was leaving at 5:00 P.M. and sailing for nine days at sea before reaching the first port, Bora Bora. If the cases had not arrived before sailing, the next practical port for them to be sent would have been Tahiti. The airline was made aware of the situation and of the passengers' business and social position. Immediately, an intensive search was made for the missing pieces. Fortunately, they were found in San Francisco and flown down to Los Angeles.

The captain had to delay sailing until the baggage arrived. Hundreds of friends and well-wishers had to stand around for another hour looking at each other. Most of the streamers had already been thrown, and tired arms sagged after waving extended good-byes. The gangway had been taken up to enable us to get moving as soon as the suitcases arrived. I had informed the passengers why we were delayed. It was, therefore, no surprise to hear a great cheer going up from passengers and friends alike as soon as the small truck with the cases was sighted.

The ship was still tied up to the dock, and the gangway entrance was open, ready to receive the cases. The agent brought the cases to the dockside and reached over the gap between the dock and the ship with the first suitcase. It was obvious that this method of loading was not practical. His arms were not long enough, and the gap too wide. So we rigged a rope on a pulley in the entrance of the gangway and handed the end of the rope to the agent. He wound it around both cases, securing them through the handles. Easing them off the dock, the cases were swung over the gap toward the waiting arms of a seaman on the ship. For some reason, the cases were not quite lined up with the gangway entrance and crashed against the side of the ship, forcing the cases to swing back to the dock, the impact causing one case to extricate itself from the ropes and fall between the ship and the dock, straight into the murky water below. The sound of it hitting the water was accompanied by gasps from all of us and screams from the owner.

The shock of seeing this ghastly happening distracted the seaman who was holding the rope. His grasp of both the rope and the situation caused him to pull on the rope. This brought the remaining suitcase back toward the ship. Unfortunately, such sudden movement gave rise to its being jerked away from the rope, and it speedily followed its predecessor into the water.

The ensuing scene made us all proud. Two dockers,

11

realizing that the recovery of these two suitcases would make them rich beyond their wildest dreams, acted with amazing speed. One went down a ladder that was attached to the dock and, upon reaching the water, grabbed one case. The other docker was lowered by a pulley on a rope between the dock and the ship. From the gangway, a boat hook appeared and was lowered to the docker on the rope. Eventually, both suitcases were retrieved, greeted by another cheer from the assembled company. It was the most eventful sailing from Los Angeles I can remember.

I am sorry to say that many of the gowns had been water damaged. However, there were some in a wearable condition, though not before our laundry had worked on them. We managed to get the lady through the first fortnight of the cruise dressed in a manner to which she was accustomed. Naturally, the company recompensed the passenger to her satisfaction, and, on our arrival in Sydney, Australia, the fashion houses reported an unexpected boom in sales.

As we continue our journey through the port passenger terminal, let us assume that all is well with your bags. The porters have taken them to the conveyor belt, while you are directed inside the terminal to book in with the Purser's Office staff. You hand them your ticket, and they check it against the passenger list. They might also wish to see evidence of your nationality and, in some cases, to take your passport. The reason for this is that at every port when the immigration officials arrive it is not unusual for them to ask to see all passports. If the ship's officials didn't take yours, it would mean that you would have to get up early at every port and bring your passport to the Purser's Office. Immigration may not clear the ship until every passport is seen. Can you imagine the resulting chaos and the time that that could take? Trying to find people on the ship later on in the cruise is not easy. Passengers are moved for all sorts of reasons, some for reasons that should be obvious to "Love Boat" viewers.

After booking in, you will first go through a security scanner, then proceed to the gangway, where the ship's photographers will greet you and ask if they can take your picture sporting your best smile to match theirs. Please do not say no; it will break their hearts. They know you may have flown thousands of miles, you're dead tired, and your hair is a mess; but you'll get more fun out of showing that picture to your friends than many others you might take. You are under no obligation to buy a picture, so always give them a chance to take one. It might be your best ever.

At the top of the gangway, you will be greeted by a member of the staff and a senior member of the Housekeeping Department. They will hand you over to a stewardess or steward. He or she will take you to your cabin, where they will acquaint you with the air conditioning, lights, etc. On your dressing table will be a great deal of information about the ship. You will possibly find a card from the maître d' giving you your assigned table number and meal sitting. Your steward or stewardess will also welcome you with a name card.

It is important to read that day's program as there may be something you are being asked to do, such as filling out a special form for the next port or seeing the maître d' for table assignments. If you arrived on board early, your luggage might already be in the cabin. If you arrived later, it might take some time. With many ladies bringing enough clothes for six months on a short seven-day cruise, it is possible to have as many as 2,500 bags to distribute among seven hundred passengers. Your bags might not be delivered until after sailing. However, if you saw them at the ship's passenger terminal, you should have nothing to worry about.

Now, what is the first thing you should do? If the bags have arrived, or some of them (they do not always come together), you should unpack. Remember, not all ships were built for world cruising. A lot of new ships, especially those built for shorter cruises, do not have the closet and drawer space of the older ships. If you don't have enough room, then I suggest you leave some of the clothes and other items you won't need for a few days in your suitcase. When you have finished with the first set of clothes, you can pack them in place of the others you are going to wear. If you are clever, you will have packed everything away again before the last day. This procedure will allow you to spend that last afternoon enjoying the sun, the deck, or the slot machines in the casino.

If your luggage has not yet arrived, my suggestion is to start reading the printed information regarding the ship. You will probably find a booklet titled, "Know Your Ship" or "Ship's Directory." Take your time, relax on your bed, and read it carefully. To make the cruise more enjoyable, it really helps to know the many and varied services offered on board. Also, it will tell you whom to contact and where to go for questions, problems, or in an emergency. Make sure you look at the shore-excursion brochure. You can enjoy seeing what the line is offering in the various ports of call. A plan of the ship is always in the package. Ships are not easy places to get around in. We employed a magician once who had never worked on a ship. I took him around when he first boarded and showed him the two showrooms where he would be performing. Three days later, he was due on for the early show at 6:45 P.M.. He never made it. Eventually, we found him in the forward bar, completely lost. He had been too embarrassed to ask where the show was taking place.

When you have finished reading everything, take the map with you and explore the ship. Most ships will have signs close to the elevators. They tell you, YOU ARE HERE. It is sometimes just as difficult to find out where YOU ARE HERE is.

Be careful as you walk around. Ships are built with safety very much in mind. You will come across WATCH YOUR STEP signs everywhere! There are risers on the *decks* (the floors) to act as buffers for the water and fire doors. Your bathroom also has a *riser* (a step) to prevent any water overflow when the ship moves. You will probably get into the habit of stepping over the riser, so much so that on arriving home you will step over air to get into your own bathroom. If you are tall, be careful of the low door frames for the fire doors along the corridors.

As you make your way around the ship, you might have to ask a crew member to confirm where something is. They will probably say, "Oh, that's on the starboard side." At this point, I should explain some of the nautical terms used on board.

Starboard is right as you face the sharp end, the *prow*. It derives comes from *steerboard*, a term used before rudders were invented, when the guy at the stern (back) had a board to steer the boat with. You cannot steer a boat in that manner on the side you wish to dock; therefore, the left-hand side is called *port*. There are four letters in the word *left* and four in *port*, which makes it easy to remember. One of the few places today where you can still see a *steerboard* being used is in Venice. The gondolier uses it on his romantic form of water transport.

On board ship, you are not walking on the floor; you are walking on the *deck*. Beside you is not a wall, but a *bulkhead*. When climbing stairs, you are going up a *companionway* (or *gangway*). Most things on board a vessel have different names from those you are used to, but land terms are quite acceptable, unless you are a sailor. I like the story of a young sailor

15

boy joining his first ship. He arrived late at the dock and rushed up the gangway, across the deck, around the bulkhead, crashing into the chief officer. The sailor picked himself up and apologized nervously. "I'm terribly sorry, sir, I didn't see you around the wall."

The officer looked at him in amazement. "Did you say 'wall,' young man?" he cried. "That's not a wall; that's a *bulkhead*." Then, pointing to the floor, he said, "And this is a *deck*. The stairs you came running up is a *gangway*. And if I ever hear you use a nonnautical term again, I will throw you straight through one of those little round windows."

Returning to your own grand tour, make sure you are on the open deck in time to watch the ship sail. This is an event not to be missed. The nearer you get to the forward part (the *prow*) of the ship, the better. Here, you will be able to see the captain on the bridge at work with the pilot, maneuvering the ship out from the dock. The pilot is also a captain and is employed by the harbor authorities to assist your ship's captain in navigating the ship in and out of the harbor. The pilot's knowledge of currents, tides, and local conditions adds to the safe operation of bringing a ship in and out of the port.

As the ship moves away into the harbor, the time is approaching when one of the most important events in cruising is about to take place, dinner. Food is very plentiful on ships. They feed and water you every two hours. Many people come on as passengers and leave as cargo. It is the abundance of calories dressed up in the most attractive way that swells the figure. However, there are plenty of healthy foods on board for those passengers who enjoy the "lean and light" way of eating.

The first evening's dress code is always casual. This is because many passengers arrive on board late, and the ship's sailing is close to dinnertime for those assigned to the first sitting. In your cabin, you will have seen on the card from the maître d' the sitting to which you have been assigned. Most ships have two sittings for meals in the dining room. For dinner, 6:00 P.M. and 8:15 P.M. seem to be the choice of most cruise ships. The first sitting is usually the most popular on shorter cruises.

On the form you filled out when you booked the cruise, you should have stated your preference. Do not be surprised if you are assigned to the second sitting when you asked for first. With seven hundred passengers on board, it is possible for over five hundred to request the first sitting. Most rooms have only four hundred places. Don't be too disappointed; the second sitting does have its advantages. The maître d' usually has much more room to maneuver in, and it is easier to deal with passengers' requests for tables and other changes. You can spend additional time in port during the morning, especially when the sailing is early afternoon. You can relax after a day in port or on deck in the sun without having to come in and immediately change for dinner. Cocktail time is much more relaxed, as is the dining. You do not have to rush your meal to move out for the next sitting. The show will be far more comfortable to watch, and you won't have to make a mad dash to get a seat. However, last week a passenger mentioned an advantage for the first sitting I had not previously heard. "We always choose first sitting so we have plenty of room in our tummies for the late-night buffet."

The maître d' is responsible for the dining room and, with headwaiters and many other waiters, has one of the toughest jobs on the ship. I wouldn't have such a job for all the tea in China (and I've been told there's a lot there). It is very important for you to enjoy your table companions (I don't mean to eat them). There are few thing worse than having to eat a meal with people you have nothing in common with or dislike. Food is not meant to be digested under such conditions. The maître d', with very little information, sometimes just by looking at names and nationality, has to put people together. Some lines ask passengers to fill out a registration form giving their age, occupation, etc. This gives the maître d' a better chance of creating an interesting and enjoyable table.

It is wise on that first night to be tolerant and understanding of your table companions. You are all in the same boat (pun intended), all tired from traveling many hours. Some may have come late, not having been able to change or shower. Their bags may not have arrived yet, and to make matters worse, they may not have the sitting or the table that they or you wanted. In other words, nobody is his or her normal, relaxed self. You probably don't like the looks of anybody, and they are thinking the same about you. And to top it all off, most of them are old. (You happen to be eighty-three.)

Do not fly to the maître d' after the meal to stand in line with the other hundred or so waiting to change their tables. You might, unfortunately, lose by the trade and do worse. Take my advice and wait until the next evening. After a day at sea, everything will look better, even the cruise director. That second evening will be formal for the captain's welcome aboard cocktail party. People will be dressed in their best, we hope, and, after a few drinks, a different person will emerge. Now is the time to judge your table companions. You will be surprised at how different they seem. Those "old" people have traveled far and are a lot more interesting to talk to than the forty-year-old couple who have never been anywhere and are taking their first cruise.

Getting back to the first night out, make sure you see the introductory show. This is when the cruise director introduces the staff and people who are going to make this vacation your best ever. The cruise director will give you information about the ship in an entertaining manner. There might well be an act in the show, followed by a welcome dance party, with prizes and champagne.

When all this is done, you can go and see what the late-night buffet has to offer. This event has become a set procedure on many ships. Some make quite a show of it with ice carvings and a very artistic food presentation. However, for the last few years, it has become very noticeable that, with the growing emphasis on diet and fitness, fewer passengers attend this feast. Still, it's a great place to meet the entertainers, staff, and musicians. Because of the shows, they had to eat early in the evening. The late-night buffet was originally served on the great liners crossing the Atlantic. They would offer it only after there had been bad weather during the day. Since nighttime often saw calmer seas, the late-night buffet availed passengers of food they had not been able to eat or, possibly, keep down during the day.

After viewing the buffet, it is time now to go to bed. But before you retire, you must take a walk around the promenade deck. Listen, as you stroll, to the romantic sound of the sea as it brushes against the ship's hull. Lean over the rail at the aft end and watch the wake in white turmoil as it stretches away into the moonlight. At this moment, as time appears to stand still, you will suddenly realize how different this is from any other vacation you have ever experienced.

Returning to your cabin all starry-eyed and romantically inclined, you must do one other thing before going to sleep. Read the next day's daily program. Then, as you waft into slumber, you can dream about all the events for the next day the good-looking, hard-working, and talented cruise director and his staff have prepared for you.

A day at sea allows the cruise director to show his paces in regard to the number of attractions he can produce to make sure you are not bored. Naturally, like anything else, you only get what you pay for. Not every ship can produce the same quality of entertainment or enrichment programs. Basically, all ships have deck sports, indoor-game competitions, keeping-fit exercise programs, etc. Many people who have never cruised think they will be bored when the itinerary reads a "day at sea."

You might be interested to read how I programmed a day at sea. I think you will agree that, with the ammunition given to me by the company, I was able to fire off a very busy day. A cruise should be as busy or as lazy as you wish. The most important thing a cruise director must do is make sure the passengers are never bored by a lack of activities. This is a typical Sunday at sea on a forty-seven-day South Seas cruise from Los Angeles to Australia and back.

DAILY PROGRAM

Sunrise 6:10 A.M./Sunset 8:05 P.M.—en route to Tonga

Dress Formal

Good Morning

6:30 A.M.	Early Risers Coffee Club meet Bob
7:30 A.M.	Fred Goerner's "Good Morning" radio show
8:00 A.M.	Fitness Follies with Doug
8:00 A.M.	Barbara's quiz available
8:30 A.M.	Catholic Mass celebrated with Father Carpenter
9:00 A.M.	Stretchasize with Doug

9:00 A.M.	Deck Sports Equipment available
9:00 A.M.	The master's voice from the bridge
9:15 A.M.	Bridge lecture by Ken
9:15 A.M.	Morning devotionals: a story, a hymn, and a prayer with Rev. Robert Mayo
9:15 A.M.	Library assistance and indoor games from Barbara
9:30 A.M.	Barbara's daily riddle available
9:30 A.M.	Sign up for tours of the navigation bridge
10:00 A.M.	Backgammon competition continues
10:00 A.M.	Shuffleboard competition for ladies
10:00 A.M.	The Bloody Mary Club meets in the Neptune Bar
10:30 A.M.	Barbara's interview with Jerry Adler
10:30 A.M.	Sign up for today's blackjack tournament
10:45 A.M.	Mileage pool: guess the day's run with Peter
11:00 A.M.	Barbara's walkathon
11:00 A.M.	Celebrity host Donald O'Connor talks about "Dancing My Way to Hollywood"
11:30 A.M.	Doug's volleyball match in the pool

Good Afternoon

12:00 P.M.	Sing-along with Andrew at the piano
12:10 P.M.	The answer to Barbara's riddle

12:15 P.M.	Derek's voice from the bridge
12:20 P.M.	Barbara's Interest Corner: calling all pilots
2:00 P.M.	Duplicate bridge with Ken
2:00 P.M.	Casino Royale opens for complimentary lessons
2:15 P.M.	Sign up for tours of the control room
2:15 P.M.	At the movies: Donald O'Connor introduces his *Singin' in the Rain*
2:30 P.M.	Aquasize with Doug in the pool
2:30 P.M.	The art of calligraphy with Peter
2:30 P.M.	Backgammon for beginners with Derek
2:30 P.M.	Barbara's Needlework Club meets
3:00 P.M.	Blackjack tournament starts
3:15 P.M.	Health consultations with Doug
3:45 P.M.	Andrew Cooke plays his teatime melodies
3:45 P.M.	Grandma's tea with Derek and Barbara
4:00 P.M.	Teatime with the family
4:15 P.M.	The answers to Barbara's quiz
4:20 P.M.	Bingo with Derek, Peter, and Barbara
5:00 P.M.	Barbara is in the library to help you
5:15 P.M.	Sunset stretch with Doug by the smokestack
5:15 P.M.	Enrichment lecture: "The Friendly Islands" with His Royal Highness Prince Tupoutoa of Tonga

Good Evening

6:00 P.M.	Fred Goerner's radio show with news-views-music
6:30 P.M.	Early evening cocktail music with Andrew
6:45 P.M.	Comedy radio: Bud Abbott and Lou Costello
6:45 P.M.	The Venus Lounge presents

THE EARLY EVENING CLASSICAL RECITAL

with

the celebrated guitarist

Terrence Farrell

6:45 P.M.	Dancing to Royal Viking Sextet in the Bergen Lounge
8:45 P.M.	A Piano interlude with Andrew
9:00 P.M.	Casino Royale opens
9:00 P.M.	The Royal Viking Sextet plays for dancing
9:15 P.M.	At the movies: *Breaker Morant*
9:30 P.M.	Preshow dancing with the Royal Viking Trio
9:45 P.M.	Music with the Penthouse Four in the Venus Lounge

9:45 P.M.	Showtime

Gary Oakes and Lou Garcia's

23

mini-musical production of

South Pacific

with all the staff and entertainers

10:30 P.M.   Dancing to the Trio in the nightclub

10:45 P.M.   The sky at night with the navigator

10:45 P.M.   Dancing after the show with the Sextet

11:15 P.M.   The Galaxy Club

presents

the harmonica virtuoso

LARRY ADLER

11:45 P.M.   Continue dancing to the wee, small hours

Good night and have another great day tomorrow!

Derek Mann

The next day has dawned, and perhaps there is some movement as the ship plows its way through the waves. A ship when moving from side to side is considered to be *rolling*; when it is heading into the waves, this is called *pitching*. For those who find they are not good sailors, it is a personal preference which they dislike most. Seasickness has many remedies other than dying. Lying down flat on one's back without a pillow helps. Some people like to remedy the problem with alcohol. However, this aid to recovery is not prescribed by the medical profession.

Nowadays, many passengers arrive with those little patches behind the ear. They wear them even when riding in the taxi conveying them to the ship. Some people can't walk across a wet lawn without them. These patches work, but some ships' doctors do not prescribe them. On rare occasions they can produce side effects that make seasickness pleasant by comparison. If, when first putting them on, you experience dizziness, tingling fingers, or nausea, or you just feel rotten, take them off.

The infirmary and Purser's Office have a liberal stock of Dramamine tablets available at no cost. If all else fails and you are affected very badly, fear not. The doctor will give you a shot in the bot'. This will put you nicely to sleep for three hours or so, but, on waking, you will be able to "walk through a storm with your head held high" and not over the rail. This injection will keep you on your feet for the rest of the cruise.

All cruise ships have a hospital or infirmary. A vessel that carries more than twelve passengers must have a doctor in attendance. Some modern cruise ships carry an intensive care unit, a dialysis machine, and other advanced forms of medical equipment.

You will have noticed in your daily program that a fire and lifeboat drill will take place the morning of your first full day. Under international maritime law, you must attend. You will find your life jacket either under your bed or in the closet. The instructions to put it on and the place where your lifeboat station or assembly station is will be located behind your cabin or closet door. When you hear the alarm bells, you will be instructed to go up on deck to your boat or assembly station. Do not go there with the tie ends of your life jacket dragging on the deck. Make sure you put the jacket on properly in the cabin. It is very easy for you and other passengers to trip over the tie ends. They are long because they have to fit all, and some of the "all" can be pretty big.

Elevators are not used in an emergency because they could be affected by power failures. Crew members will help you find your way to your lifeboat station, and an officer will tell you the procedures followed in an emergency. It is the practice of many ships to lower the boats in order for you to see the operation. The drill can take some time, but it is worth it. I remember one of the passengers once saying to an officer, "If the ship is sinking, do we have to stand here as long as this?" The officer's answer is not recorded.

It is possible that after this drill there will be a talk on the tours and ports of call by the cruise director or the shore excursion manager. Even if you are not going on a tour, it is important to know about the places you are visiting. Countries have different cultures, and it's nice to know the local customs and the places of interest. If you are in doubt about the choice of a tour, I suggest you take the city tour. This can act as a preview that lets you see what the call offers. In the afternoon, there might be another tour to somewhere else, or you can go back into town and visit an area where you would prefer to spend more time. In fact, part of cruising is very much a preview of countries and ports. If you fall in love with a place, you can go back and enjoy a full vacation another time.

Once you have bought the tour of your choice, make sure you are on the pier at the time stated in the ship's daily program. A lot of tour companies do not refund the cost of the tour ticket if you miss the tour. Only if you are ill and have a note from the ship's doctor or if the tour is canceled for whatever reason by the ship or tour operator is a refund given.

Some passengers get very upset when they see the tour passengers getting off first. They think it is because they have paid more. That is not the case. The tour operators on land have schedules to keep with other ships and land tourists. In the U.S. Virgin Islands, at the popular port of Saint Thomas, there can be as many as eight cruise ships docked at the same time, all using the same operator. With only so many buses, boats, etc., timing is very important to keep the tour operation running smoothly.

Unhappily, a ship will not always be able to dock alongside the pier. There can be three reasons for this: one of them is that there is not enough water depth to take the ship; second, the dock is already booked or taken; last, it's a matter of cost, since docking can be very expensive, as much as a quarter of a million dollars a year for a ship calling once a week. That cost all adds on to the price of a passenger ticket. A cruise ship carries *tenders,* which are built to take you to the shore in comfort. They are not lifeboats, though in an emergency they can be used in conjunction with them. Most tender rides are no longer than ten minutes and give you a good opportunity to get great photos, along with a terrific view of the size and the scope of the ship. In many cases, tenders also dock much closer to the center of town.

Make sure you don't miss the last tender back to the ship. The sailing and last tender schedule are always posted at the gangway and on the pier where the tender docks. If ever you do miss the ship, you'll personally be responsible for paying and getting yourself to the next port. The local police or harbor master will put you in touch with the ship's agent, who will arrange to get you there. However, if you are on a ship's tour, and it somehow misses the ship, you are not liable for any expenses. One other consideration regarding being off the ship. In many Third World countries, some taxis are not insured for your injuries, whereas all tour operators contracted by the cruise companies are. This is important to remember when considering your land tours.

At this point, I must tell you about an incident involving a passenger who did miss the ship. We were cruising Alaska and had arrived in Juneau, its capital. The dock was occupied, so we anchored out. The passengers were taken by tender into town. Another cruise ship, the *Prinzendam*, was docked where the tender was moored. It was a much smaller ship than our *Royal Viking Star* and quite different in shape and color. The time had come for us to sail, the anchor was weighed, taken up, and we made our way back down the Gastineau Channel en route to our next call, Glacier Bay. Just before dinner, I received a call from the purser's desk telling me that a lady had reported the loss of her sister, a Miss Pearson. She apparently was not on board, so I was asked if I could make a check of our areas. They had a picture of her at the desk. I got my hostess and assistant to help me in the search. We started off looking in the cinema, then in the chapel (yes, we had a chapel in those days), and later in the public rooms. After only ten minutes, I got a call over the public address system to go to the radio room. It was the cruise director from the *Prinzendam*, still docked in Juneau.

"Derek, I've got one of your flock on my ship," he said.

"It's not a Miss Pearson, is it?" I inquired.

"It sure is," he responded.

"What's she doing there?" I asked.

"She thought this was her ship," he said.

"But we were anchored out, and you were docked," I said incredulously.

"She walked on the ship and apparently went to the bar. She's had a few drinks. The barman remembers her watching your ship sail," he said with a laugh.

"Then how did she find out it was the wrong ship?" I asked.

"She couldn't find her cabin. We don't have a number 355, and that's the number on her key. I'll hand her over to the agent, and he can get her back to you. I doubt if they can get her to Glacier Bay, so you'll probably see her in Skagway."

I immediately got the purser to inform Miss Pearson's

sister. She had the same reaction we did, relieved but bewildered to know how her sister could have possibly mistaken our ship for theirs. We contacted the agent, and he told us she would be joining us early in the morning with the national park rangers in Glacier Bay. On these visits to Glacier Bay, the rangers are customarily our guests on board and provide the passengers with information, books, and a slide show. In addition, one of them is usually on the bridge, giving a commentary on the wonderful sights that abound in this spectacular part of Alaska.

Miss Pearson arrived on schedule at Bartlett Cove, in a helicopter no less, before boarding the rangers' launch. The only thing I could get out of her was the fact that the journey had cost her two hundred dollars and a great deal of embarrassment.

I mentioned the chief purser in my opening remarks. This officer is the ship's accountant, also responsible for all the official and legal paperwork required by customs and immigration to clear the ship. The Purser's Office is the information center of the ship. This is where you bring questions and problems that cannot be solved by a steward or stewardess. The chief purser deals with room changes and all monetary matters, such as changing travelers' checks, buying stamps, and providing cash boxes. To work in that office, it is sometimes necessary to have the patience of Job. But they are special people, trained to be patient and understanding of passengers' needs, complaints, and problems. If your problem is not being dealt with to your satisfaction, you can arrange an appointment with the chief purser or hotel manager. The captain is not the person to ask. Only if a very serious situation arises is the captain ever involved with passengers' problems.

Some of the requests and questions asked at the desk are priceless. One summer, the ship was going to Honningvag on the northern tip of Norway. From there we were going to the island of Spitsbergen, only eight hundred miles from the North Pole. The captain decided we would go even farther north to see if we could meet the Arctic Sea ice fields.

We had left Spitsbergen and were making our way in a calm, ice-cold sea when a lady came to the Purser's Office.

"May I have some of those Dramamine things?" she asked.

"Are you seasick?" the purser inquired. "The sea is very calm today."

"Oh, it's not the sea," she said. "It's the altitude that's affecting me. I've never been this far north before."

The purser gave her the tablets and smiled, assuring her that she would feel better once we started to go south. That's called being understanding.

To really enjoy the cruise, it is important that you do not harbor a complaint or anything that gets you angry or upset. The cruise director and Purser's Office are there to help in this area. Always try to find out the reason that a particular situation is upsetting you. After four days into one cruise, a passenger burst into my office. He was livid, his face red with anger, and his voice shaking in fury.

"How dare you let these people on tour get off before us?" he demanded. "Just because they have paid for a tour does not give them the right to shorten our day in this port."

I explained to him the reason (as I did earlier in this chapter). He accepted my explanation with calm and understanding. For three days that poor man had been fuming about the tours ruining his cruise. However, I must say, in my experience there are some who get no pleasure from a vacation unless there is something to gripe about. Fortunately, such people are few and far between.

One lady comes to mind who first showed her face at the reception desk one hour after sailing on a world cruise.

We shall call her Mrs. Edwards. In her hand she had a list that looked as if it had been written over a period of many cruises. She was a single and sharing a cabin with a lady she did not know. In addition, her dining room table was not by the window, nor was she seated alone, as she had requested.

"I have a physical disability that makes it uncomfortable for people to watch me eat," she said. (That was a new one!)

She insisted on being moved to a cabin on her own at no extra cost. "Please make sure that the cabin you move me to is close to an elevator. I have trouble walking." The list went on and on.

Finally, she insisted on having dinner at least once with the captain.

The next day she excelled herself. At the beauty salon, she told the operator that this was her seventh world cruise on the *Rotterdam*. She happened to be on the *Royal Viking Star*. The operator told her, after much persuasion, that she was on a different ship. Mrs. Edwards promptly left the salon and descended on the Purser's Office, demanding to be put off at the next port.

The hotel manager decided to phone her son, whose name was on the passenger registration form as next of kin. He was a lawyer of some note in Washington. Her son explained that his mother had been on the *Rotterdam* several times but had had difficulty this year in making a booking. He had told his mother of the problem, and she had been perfectly agreeable to the change. Her son spoke to her, and, after a few minutes with her saying little, she passed the phone back to the hotel manager. The son more or less pleaded with the hotel manager not to let her leave the ship. It became rather obvious that the *Rotterdam* had had enough of Mrs. Edwards.

The passengers were getting fed up with her continual

moaning. We tried to understand, but she never stopped reiterating how much better it was on the *Rotterdam*.

Throughout the cruise, her complaints never ceased. One evening Fred Goerner produced a great show he had written for the cruise, "Memories of Jeanette MacDonald and Nelson Eddy." They are long dead, but their music lives on. The show was a great success and was followed by an enthusiastic standing ovation.

After the performance, I bought the company a drink, then made my way through the lounge. There by the door was Mrs. Edwards. She slowly walked toward me with a frown, and, putting her face close to mine, she said in an aggravated fashion, "If that show had been on the *Rotterdam*, they would have been the real people!" (Back alive at Mrs. Edwards's insistence?)

At the end of the cruise (a world cruise, mind you), many passengers made written complaints about Mrs. Edwards to the effect that their cruise had not been enhanced by her presence. The company was forced into the decision of not accepting any application she might make to sail with us again.

A year later, the *Royal Viking Star* was sailing to Alaska out of Los Angeles. I was on the gangway greeting our passengers when well back in the line I saw Mrs. Edwards. The hotel manager was not on board, so I phoned the captain and told him who was waiting in line to come on board.

"Don't let that bloody woman on this ship," was his curt command.

I decided to walk down the gangway and take her aside. "Hello, Mrs. Edwards. How are you?"

"I'm afraid you're mistaken. I'm not Mrs. Edwards. My name is Mrs. Phillips, and who are *you?*" she said indignantly.

"Come along now, Mrs. Edwards. You know who I am."

I explained to her that the captain did not want her on board. "You were so unhappy here last time. Why have you come back?" I asked.

She didn't tell me. Turning to the assembled long line of passengers, she proceeded to tell them about the problem. When she started to comment on the unmarried status of the captain's parents at the time of his birth, I called over a port security officer. After explaining our predicament, I left to continue greeting a lot of bemused passengers.

Half an hour later, I was in the office when I received a call from the Neptune Bar. There was a woman causing a problem. She was getting up a petition. "Something about staying on board," the barman said.

I decided to call the captain. This was a job for the officer of the watch. Apparently, a couple of passengers had taken pity on Mrs. Edwards and managed to get her a visitor's pass, but we somehow maneuvered her off the ship and back on the dock.

She was still on the dock as we sailed, shouting obscenities about the captain, me, and the line. I watched her leave the pier. It's a pity she didn't stay. The *Rotterdam* was due in that dock the very next day.

*   *   *

Returning to this first evening at sea, you will have the pleasure that night of meeting the captain at his Welcome Aboard cocktail party. He will receive you at the door of the main lounge. When you arrive, you will be greeted by the hostess. It is not correct to be introduced holding a drink in one hand and a cigarette in the other. Give the hostess your name, and she will introduce you to the captain. While shaking his hand, you might have your photograph taken before being shown to a seat by a member of the staff. When the captain has finished receiving all the passengers, he will introduce his senior officers and department heads. It is not good etiquette to leave the lounge until he has done so and the cruise director has thanked him.

There is no restriction on the amount you may drink at the party or, on most ships, the amount of food you may consume at mealtimes. However, when, after a few days, you find yourself with digestive upsets half the night, don't think you have been poisoned or there's a bug going round the ship. Your little tummy isn't used to all the food and drink you have been supplying it with over the last few days, and it's telling you it would like a breather.

Food remains the number one occupation on a ship. But though most ships may still "feed and water you" every two hours, over the last few years, drinking has gone out of fashion. Last year, one bar manager said to me, "We don't see a respectable drunk anymore." In this last year, I can remember seeing only one passenger who you could have described as being drunk. Twenty years ago, every day you could have seen many a lost soul under the influence. Passengers would occupy the same bar stool at the Lido bar from its opening at ten in the morning till its closing. They used to call the bar their office. So I made it just that. I gave each of them a telephone, a desk pad, a pen, and their very own nameplate. Later in the day, they were usually helped back to their cabins by friendly bar waiters.

On one South Seas cruise, lasting forty-seven days, four of the resident bar-stool members actually left the ship—but only once. That was in Sydney, Australia, where they went to visit a few local bars, doubtless to "foster" better relations between their states and the inhabitants of New South Wales.

Today, far more passengers prefer wine, and the hard-spirit drinkers are becoming a rare breed. It is this more sober, more receptive group who usually attend and enjoy the first big show on the ship immediately following the captain's Welcome Aboard dinner. The show is customarily the production company's presentation. In most cases, you will find it a very good show, designed to entertain all tastes. Of course, there will always be those whom one can never please. Even so illustrious a celebrity as Oscar Peterson, the jazz pianist, failed to entice one couple on the *Royal Viking Star*. They had wandered in from the aft deck and might have attained an unwelcome glimpse of the redoubtable pianist in his skivvies had I not politely but firmly guided them away from the dressing room area, asking if they would be so kind as to use another route. "Mr. Peterson is changing for his concert," I explained.

"Who's Mr. Peterson?" asked the husband.

"Oscar Peterson is a very famous pianist," I replied.

"Never heard of him," said the wife.

"We're not fond of Mozart and that sort of thing," stated the husband.

I informed them that Mr. Peterson was a jazz pianist.

"Oh God, that's even worse," they retorted and quickly left the scene.

Ultimately, all entertainers on board have to live with their audiences. Not all artists are used to this or indeed like it. Most artists come to the theater, enter by the stage door, do their show, leave by the same entrance, and go home. They do not have to hear, "Why don't you sing some more? Your jokes are awful," or "My son's got a much better voice than you. Where should he write to get a job here?" or last, "Besides this, what do you do for a living?"

That is why a lot of acts do not like cruising. In addition, some entertainers get seasick, and it's not easy to do a show with that problem.

All good things must come to an end, and now, let's say, the last day has arrived. The Purser's Office will have contacted you earlier in the cruise, asking for your disembarkation details. Cruise lines have different ways of dealing with the disembarkation process, so I won't go into them here. Sufficient to say, the important thing to do is to go to the disembarkation talk given by the cruise director or shore excursion manager. They will cover every detail of leaving the ship and also the Customs and Immigration formalities.

All of us have our own way of dealing with that important talk. I like to greet my passengers by asking, "Is there anyone here from out of town?" By that time, they all feel at home and part of the family, so the shout goes up, "No," followed hopefully by laughter. If I don't get either, I have a good idea of what the comment sheets are going to look like. Most lines provide these forms, but many passengers do not bother to fill them out. They think that if they say something bad, their evaluation will disappear into the wastepaper basket.

This is not the case with most cruise lines today. In many cases, the hotel manager, or another senior officer, will hold the key to the comments box. If the line operates this card system properly, the passenger would see that the most practical suggestions and any problems are dealt with immediately before the new passengers arrive for the next cruise. The card is not a complaint sheet, although they should be mentioned. It is hoped that you will have already dealt with any complaints during the cruise; so the comment sheet is also a suggestion sheet and a chance to show, by your checks, how the ship's departments and services have performed and to mention anyone who has given particularly good service. Many good ideas that have improved the programs and operation of the ship have come from passengers.

I continue my talk by mentioning the suggested tipping figure. Once again, the figure changes from line to line. For your room steward and dining room server, an approximate figure of fifty dollars per week per person is fairly common. As I say, it is a suggested figure. You can give more or less, depending on the quality or amount of service you expect or demand. Therefore, it is good to include these figures when working out your budget for the cruise.

As to baggage, this must be put out before you go to bed, usually before 12:00 A.M. Make sure the correct tags are on and you have left something out to wear for the morning. You may laugh, but on one occasion., in Fort Lauderdale, Florida, I received a telephone call from a distressed lady. She said her husband was standing in his underpants with nothing else to wear. She had gone to bed early and left a note for him to close the bags and put them outside. He had been enjoying a few last drinks in the casino and arrived back at the cabin late and rather the worse for wear. Seeing the note, he took off his clothes, packed them in the suitcase, and, with the others, put them outside the door to be collected. I took her down to the customs shed, where we managed to retrieve his bag and dress the poor guy.

That last morning, before the ship is cleared, passengers will have to deal with Customs and Immigration. Here again, the procedure changes from port to port and country to country. The cruise director will tell you how it is going to operate. One thing is definite: you will have to be up early on that last day. The cabin stewards will be grateful to you for clearing your cabin after the early breakfast. They have to completely clean the cabin for the new passengers arriving that afternoon. You can relax until you are called, usually either by deck, number, or card color, in the public rooms. Never go to the gangway until you are called. Officials and especially baggage handlers get very upset when individuals block the gangway area.

Customs officers in the United States are very fair and do their job in an efficient, professional manner. However, they come down hard if you don't declare what you should. Some people wonder how they are able to pick out that one person who has tried to beat the system. You might think it's the constant wiping of sweat from the brow, the clammy hand run down the trouser or skirt, or the nervous twitch of the right eye. It has nothing to do with any of these. It is the unusual tremor of the Adam's apple. If they see that moving, you've had it. That is why many of the ship's shops have a sale of polo or turtleneck sweaters on the last day of the cruise.

At this point, I must relate my favorite story about customs. It involves an Irish Sister of Mercy. She had left Ireland to visit Lourdes in France. Her life's ambition had been to see the grotto and worship at the shrine of the Virgin Mary, the scene of many miracles. On her return, she arrived in Calais to take the ferry over to London before flying back to Dublin. As she was waiting in Calais, she saw a bottle of her favorite gin on the shelf of the duty-free store. Not being able to resist temptation, she bought it. In her bag was a large bottle of mineral water, a quarter full. She emptied it and replaced it with the gin. Arriving at Dublin airport, she went through customs.

"Have you anything to declare, Sister?" the Customs officer asked.

"No, I have not," she replied.

"What's in the bottle?" she was asked.

"Oh," she said, "that's holy water from Lourdes."

"Well, fancy that," said the customs officer. Then, taking it, the officer unscrewed the top and smelt it. Slowly looking up, he said seriously, "Sister, this is not holy water. This is gin."

The sister looked up toward heaven and, in a voice filled with emotion, cried out, "Glory be to God, another miracle!"

One last point. When you eventually walk down the

way to collect your bags from the customs shed, please have your customs form made out, signed, and in your hand. The thing you most want to do is get home. Any delays will make you frustrated and upset, far more so than when coming to the ship. You would not believe the time that is taken by people trying to find the customs form, when, just at the gate, you have to give it to the customs officer. It becomes a comedy when the husband is asked for the form by the customs officer. He starts to look for it; then, turning to his wife, he says, "Have you got the form, dear?"

"No, my love, I gave it to you."

"No, you didn't, sweetheart. I put it on the desk for you. Remember, it said it had to be signed by the head of the family."

"Yes, I signed it, dear; then I gave it back to you."

"Are you sure it's not in your purse?"

And so it goes, with the customs officer tapping his foot and looking, patently irritated, around him. The husband is still frantically looking through all his pockets, eventually finding the form in a back pocket he never knew he had. We did a time and motion study in New Orleans a few years ago. One week we told the passengers nothing about keeping the form out, the next week we did. By mentioning the procedure with the same number of passengers, it took fourteen fewer minutes than the week before.

At the end of my talk, I ask passengers with any questions to see me outside my office. So often hundreds of passengers have to listen to questions, half of which have already been answered, and the other half of a personal nature that are of no interest to anybody else. By seeing passengers individually, it adds a personal touch and releases all the others to go about their business, let alone releasing the lounge for another activity.

The last evening is always an emotional one. Many new

friends have been made and addresses and telephone numbers exchanged. After the captain's farewell dinner, the cruise director produces his farewell show, and you start to think of next year. We hope it will be another cruise. The next day will be a long one. Most passengers will retire early; others will make a long night of it. But when tomorrow comes, they will take home many memories, helped by the photos—and souvenirs—of a vacation like no other.

Not all cruise lines will operate as I have described. There can be big differences when you pay big bucks. But basically most ships conform to traditional practices, such as captains' parties, etc. One sitting for dinner is a joy for passenger and crew alike. Passengers come together more readily when not segregated by this unfortunate procedure. But you do not find this one-sitting arrangement on most popular cruise ships. It is a pleasure enjoyed mostly by the up-scale market.

Before closing this chapter, I would like to expand on the duties of a cruise director. The job is important in ways beyond just keeping you all happy. In fronting the ship, attitude and presentation can color the atmosphere of a cruise. I once watched a cruise director destroy a cruise on the very first night with his attitude and bad humor. The ship's top management relies on the cruise director to set an exact tone to correspond with how the owners would wish their image to be presented in the marketplace.

Many apply for the position of cruise director. The job, as previously mentioned, has an image of glamour and romance. My friend Brian Beaton was the entertainment manager for the Royal Viking Line, and I shall be eternally grateful to him for giving me my first job as a cruise director. Brian received many applications every month for the position. He decided to compile this letter and send it in reply.

Hello!

Your inquiry, along with many others, has prompted the preparation of this standard response.

The duties and responsibilities of a cruise director may vary slightly with each line, depending on its needs, but the following applies to the Royal Viking Line.

He must have many talents, and a basic background in the specialized knowledge of theater arts, the same that the director of a play requires: set design, construction, lighting techniques, costume design and makeup, staging, timing, and overall direction and production. A major duty is the production and creation of a varied entertainment program. Also, the cruise director may be a performer himself, and most are. The cruise director has to work with the talents of his staff and the entertainers assigned to the ship. He must be able to settle disputes and deal with temperamental personalities.

In addition to being a producer, the cruise director must administer the deck sports programs and host social events. He must be diplomatic and courteous at all times. The job demands that he be visible and socialize as much as possible with the passengers in helping to create a family atmosphere.

The cruise director can expect to work as long as twelve to eighteen hours a day among the planning, rehearsals, performances, socializing, and the steady flow of unexpected problems. When the ship is in its most glamorous of ports, he and the entertainment staff are found on board rehearsing for the next show. The job does not really present an opportunity to "see the world," despite the fact that it requires being away from home for months on end. Constant tensions, facing deadlines, and demands for ingenuity and flexibility, put added pressures on an already difficult job.

Hopefully, this information may answer many of your questions regarding the glamorous position of "cruise director."

I might say the job was everything Brian said it was. My average day was sixteen hours, and many ports in the world that I have been to I have never had time to see. I have had to deal with tears, fights, marital problems, unbelievable displays of temperament, death, suicide, and even murder. However, most cruise directors today do not have to have the same background as we did in earlier days. The vast majority of ships are involved in cruises of seven days or less, and, in many cases, the programs are the same week after week. Nevertheless, the pressures are still there. Although the schedule may be the same, standards have to be kept. Yet I find it far more difficult running a seven-day cruise than a fifty-day one. Keeping up the enthusiasm, not only for yourself but for the staff and entertainers around you, is a major part of the game nowadays. The cruise director's enthusiasm should shine like a beacon and create a feeling of fun, and his personality should make the passengers really feel at home and comfortable with the ship and with themselves.

What follows immediately is an odyssey I have myself traveled, and the later stories come from many ships and many cruises on which I have served.

Now, let's go cruising.

II

The First Love Boat?

It all started at a golf club in May of 1955. My friend Bob and I had just finished a successful round of golf and were enjoying the fruits of our labors at the bar, when we were joined by Bill Carter. He was a shipping man in the city of London. "How would you two guys like to go on a Mediterranean cruise this August?" he asked. It was like saying, "How would you guys like a thousand pounds?"

"That would be great, but how much will it cost?" I asked.

"Fifty-two pounds each," he said. (That was about $150 in those days.) We could not believe it was so cheap. Without hesitation, our reply was an immediate "Yes." Bill said he would send us all the details.

A month later, the cruise information arrived. I cannot remember ever being so excited over opening up an envelope. Our ship was the *Southern Cross*. It was to be its first Mediterranean cruise. The ship was built for the Australian run and had done its first voyage ever in March. The *Southern Cross* was a revolutionary vessel; the funnel and engine room were aft, allowing for passengers' decks, and a midship indoor pool. Weighing in at twenty thousand tons, this was the first passenger ship to be one-class tourist. I must have read it all ten times.

At last, that eventful day in August arrived, when we took the boat train from Waterloo to Southampton. I remember the thrill of walking up the gangway and being greeted by the purser, who was a friend of Bill's. Bob and I were made very welcome and, after leaving the purser's desk, were taken to our cabin.

There we had a surprise. It was a cabin for four and not very big. Our two roommates were a little older than we. One was a dentist; the other, a Foreign Office official. It was obvious at the start that our love life was going to be badly affected by this arrangement.

The first morning out, we managed to get a system going to carry out our ablutions. With so little room, it was a one-at-a-time job. The bathroom and toilet were down the corridor; now we knew why the cruise was so cheap. The dentist surprised us with his early morning habit. He was the last to wake and, on doing so, reached into his case and produced a bottle of Beefeater gin. He promptly put a large amount into his teacup, topping it up with just enough tea so as not to spoil the gin. He seemed to enjoy it and promptly poured himself another. By the time it came for him to get up, he couldn't. His body decided it needed more sleep. We left him blissfully snoring and went to breakfast.

On returning, his considerable form was kneeling as in prayer at the washbowl with the resulting malady of his liquid breakfast. We left and informed the steward of the situation.

At lunchtime, our dentist friend joined us at the bar and apologized for his indisposition. He informed us that his doctor had decided it would be a good idea if he got away for a couple of weeks. A cruise had been selected as a rest from his habit. Imagine a doctor suggesting a cruise to an alcoholic!

We left him there enjoying his liquid lunch and proceeded to the deck buffet. It was there that my life changed. Although I was twenty-four, love in its purest form had not yet touched my heart. For the first time, and, as it happened, the last, I fell in love at first sight. She was the most beautiful thing I had ever seen. What made it so wonderful was that the moment my eyes alighted on this vision of loveliness, her eyes met mine and she smiled.

Fortunately, I was not carrying anything at the time because I would have dropped it. I knew I had to meet her. I pointed her out excitedly to Bob. He reminded me what the chief purser had told us the night before. "I have good news for you chaps," he'd said. "There are 366 single women on this ship and only 67 single men. So don't rush into anything permanent." His warning mattered not. This one was the girl for me, and not only for that moment, but forever.

Not feeling hungry for anything else but love, I made my way over to the table where she was sitting. With her was another attractive girl, who turned out to be her friend.

"May I join you?" I pleaded.

"Please do," she replied.

My Juliet was Kate, and it was not surprising to learn that she was a fashion model. I cannot remember the details of our conversation. Suffice it to say, we got on like a house on fire. I left the table an hour later, hopelessly in love. I was truly smitten, and all Bob could do was laugh.

That evening we prepared ourselves for the night's festivities. Our dentist friend had not returned to the cabin. Doubtless, he was still at the bar. Dressed in our best, we made our way to the watering hole. The barman informed us that our dentist friend had had an accident. After a long liquid lunch, he had apparently had fallen off the stool and hurt himself. I called the purser's desk to find out how he was. They gave me the number of the hospital, and, on ringing up, I was told he would be staying there for a couple of days. I asked the nurse to give him our best and tell him we would pop in and see him next day.

After dinner, we went to the nightclub and enjoyed a very happy evening. This time, it was Bob who was a smitten by a young lady, whose profession was in the field of gynecology. Kate and I left them at the bar and took a stroll round the deck, avoiding other couples. I walked Kate to her cabin, kissed her good night, and decided to call it a day. Even though I was twenty-four, I was still naive about quite a few things. One of them was this business of men having sexual relations with each other. This was past all comprehension to me. If a man was "light on his feet," I just thought he was slightly effeminate. I did not associate it with sex. All my friends were manly and enjoyed the company of women. I had never knowingly associated with homosexuals. Arriving at my cabin, I opened the door and, as I entered, saw the most unbelievable sight. There on his bed was our Foreign Office friend, wearing the most bizarre slumber wear and smoking a cigarette in a long holder. Taking the cigarette holder slowly out of his mouth, he greeted me with a lingering smile. "Where's your friend?" he asked.

I told him Bob had found a member of the National Health Service.

"Oh, good," he said. "I'm glad we can spend some time alone together."

I still didn't catch on until he asked me if I was going to undress.

At that point, I started to feel distinctly uncomfortable—not only that, but frightened. I told him I had left my lighter at the bar and had to retrieve it. I left the cabin, flushed and embarrassed. It was now about twelve-thirty in the morning. The bar had a few people left, among the few, Bob and his lady doctor. She was sharing a cabin with three others. A place for intimacy eluded them, since all the lifeboats were claimed, as were all the elevators, which I discovered had at first been rented out by the crew at five pounds a night, the price now rising by the hour. Lovers would return the key in the morning. So Bob and she were another frustrated couple with no home they could call their own.

"What are you doing back here?" Bob asked.

I pulled him to one side and told him of the happenings in our cabin. Once again, he laughed. I went to the bar, not wishing to be a "gooseberry," and waited for Bob to finish consulting with the doctor. I certainly was not going to walk back into that cabin alone.

The next day we had a real stroke of luck. The ship's doctor informed us that the dentist would have to be confined to the hospital for the remainder of the cruise. One down, one to go.

At dinner that evening, our Foreign Office friend told us he was being upgraded. We later found out that his upgrade was to a suite occupied by a butch dry cleaner from Wandsworth in London. We now had the cabin to ourselves.

That evening at dinner, we were told the captain had ordered all outside decks to be fully lighted all night. He was rather upset that his brand new ship was being used as a copulating cruiser. Everybody seemed to be at it, except me, of course. Our love was too pure to start that lark. I was still at the "I respect you too much" stage. The furthest I had ventured was a meaningful kiss on the lips.

The next day we came to our first port, Palma. This island remains one of my favorites in the Mediterranean. We boarded the tour bus and started our grand tour. I will not bore you with all the details. Suffice it to say, we visited the Caves of the Dragon. These caves have many great caverns. All of them are festooned with stalagmites. In the largest of all the caverns, an orchestra in small boats came out from between the stalagmites, lamps swinging from their small masts. They entered playing Handel's *Water Music*. Stopping in front of seats built up like an amphitheater, they played a concert of romantic music. The last number was the "Barcarolle" ("Belle nuit, o nuit d'amour"), which they played moving slowly back between the pillars, the music fading away with no ending. Kate and I held each other's hands tightly throughout the performance.

We arrived two days later in Naples, the second of our four ports in fourteen days. I daresay that it will surprise many modern cruisers to find that we only called at four ports in fourteen days. You must remember, these were the days when cruising meant cruising, not port hopping. In Naples, Kate and her friend had prebooked a tour to the beautiful island of Capri. They would not be back till late that night. With Tommy, a new friend we had made on board, Bob and I decided to rent a car with a driver. Pompeii would be our first destination. We drove out of Naples, passing beneath Mount Vesuvius, eventually coming to this amazing relic of the Roman Empire.

We decided on a private guide. He was very presentable and showed us a letter signed by Churchill thanking him for acting as his guide. We were suitably impressed, and he certainly knew his stuff. As we were visiting the different areas of the ruined city, we came upon the Villa of the Two Brothers. They had been wealthy fishermen who seem to have shown an interest in more than fish. One wall of a room was covered with paintings of men and women in all sorts of weird positions. They were not acrobats. They were performing many positions of sexual intercourse. As I knew only three (positions, that is), I found it quite educational. I was glad Kate was not with me, as I wished to surprise her, when the time came, with my versatility. We left slightly bewildered and continued our grand tour. Next stop, Sorrento.

It was pouring rain as our little entourage made its way to this famous resort on the Italian Riviera. It was time for lunch, and our driver suggested an impressive-looking *caffe ritrovo* overlooking the town. We climbed up an attractive walled path to a wide terrace. I noticed a waiter running to the end of the veranda, where an old gramophone was sitting. He proceeded to wind it up. The strains of a very scratchy "Return to Sorrento" reached our ears, as he ran back to show us a table.

Unfortunately, most of the tables were wet, as the rain was seeping through the old canopy. However, one table, rather close to the gramophone, was dry. We were given the menu. As many of you know, Italy, like so many other countries, was experiencing a postwar depression, and food was still scarce. Nevertheless, spaghetti was available, and with a *Bolognese* sauce and a bottle of chianti, what could be better? "Return to Sorrento" continued playing. The rain never stopped and was now making its way all over the tiled floor. We decided to leave, so I asked for the bill. For four people, it worked out to a whopping fifteen dollars each, and this was 1955! I could not believe it. I looked at the bottom of the bill. There was an entertainment charge.

"What is this?" I asked.

"Oh, that, *signore,* is for the music."

"Are you talking about the gramophone?"

"*Si, signore.*"

I told him in plain English that he was barmy and that there was no way we were going to pay this bill. He would have to call the police. With that, he scratched out the tax and reduced the food price. As we left, he took off the record, making it clear he did not want us to return to his Sorrento.

The rain stopped as we were driving along Sorrento's promenade. We saw another little *caffe ritrovo* in the distance and thought how nice it would be to have a liqueur and a Neapolitan ice cream. We got out of the car, making our way onto a very rickety pier. The wood was falling apart as we watched rats by the dozen running about over the rocks beneath us. This was not the image of Sorrento that we had grown to know and love. As we were halfway along the pier, one of the waiters saw us coming (like they all saw us coming) and ran to (yes, you've guessed it) a gramophone. Once again, we were regaled with the scratchy request of returning to Sorrento. Arriving on the premises, we asked if he would kindly play the other side. Unfortunately, that was even more badly scratched than the other, so they shut it off. But they hummed it for the rest of the time we were there.

We returned by way of a cameo factory. This delicate art of Italy allowed us to buy some gifts of true quality. We drove back to Naples along the *autostrada*, badly in need of repair, still suffering from the ravages of tanks and heavy army vehicles that had traversed it some ten years before. Naples was also in bad shape. As we came back into the city through its slums, we saw children, completely naked, playing in the streets.

Back on the ship, we showered and enjoyed a few drinks. Bob and Tommy had made arrangements for our driver to pick us up and take us to a nightclub after dinner. Kate was not due back until well past eleven o'clock, so a nightclub would while away a couple of hours. I have never been a nightclub type, always balking at the ridiculous sums of money charged for drinks. However, Tommy had said the evening was on him.

After dinner, the driver picked us up at the gangway. As we drove out of the dock gates, Tommy remembered he had left his wallet in the cabin. To save us time, I said I would lend him mine. After driving along the Via Roma for a few hundred yards, we turned up a dark narrow street. Reaching the top, we turned into an even darker alley and stopped outside an old building. We got out and stood in front of two large doors. I really didn't like the look of it.

"Don't be misled by the look of the villa from outside," said the driver. He knocked on one of the two large doors. The door was slowly opened, and a snappily dressed fellow beckoned us in. In front of us was a long, sweeping staircase at the bottom of which was a wizened little lady sitting in a concierge booth. I thought she was part of the security arrangements. We were asked in broken English to follow our "gentleman" up the stairs. I did not like the feel of this at all.

I turned and caught the taxi driver by the arm, telling him, "You don't leave, and be sure you keep the engine running."

I caught up with the others as they came to two very ornate doors. They were opened by our gentleman guide, who led us into one of the most impressive rooms I had seen for a long time. It was furnished in classical Italian style. The furniture was decorated in gilt and red brocade. It all looked very expensive. Huge red velvet drapes covered very high windows, and a beautiful Persian carpet covered the entire floor. Along one side was a bar with a large glass mirror reflecting the rich decor of the room.

At this point, our gentleman guide excused himself and was then replaced a few moments later by a lady of indeterminate years. She approached us with a smile. "What would you gentlemen like to drink?" she asked in very good English.

We accepted her kind offer and ordered. I asked her who had first owned this impressive villa. Apparently, it had been built in the late part of the last century by an Italian count in the service of Victor Emmanuel II. Still, I asked her if it was now a private club. I could not understand why Bob and Tommy were laughing. They seemed to know something I did not. I was very soon to find out just what they knew. Now the lady was smiling, making all three of them seem vastly superior. The lady then asked if we would like to meet the girls. Bob and Tommy enthusiastically said, "Yes." Dawn broke, and I suddenly saw the light. We were in a brothel.

As she walked away to open a door, I said to my companions, "Why didn't you tell me?"

"We just wanted to see the expression on your face when you found out," they said with a chuckle.

"Kate will never speak to me again if she knows I went for a night out in a brothel," I said anxiously.

"Don't worry," said Bob. "It's a demonstration. They're only going to show us the positions you saw in the Villa of Two Brothers this morning."

I breathed a sigh of relief. I wasn't happy, but at least it was better than having to perform them myself.

At this point, a door opened, and in came Madame with eight of the tattiest women I have ever seen. They were wearing the skimpiest of dresses and were a most unattractive lot. Madame introduced them by name, as we smiled politely at each one. Bob stopped me from introducing ourselves. He felt it wasn't necessary. Madame asked us to choose two of them. Apparently, it was going to be a team effort. They were all shapes and sizes.

The funny side of it all struck me as we started the selection process. At one end was a rather heavy woman, and, in the center, a short skinny one. I suggested that we take Laurel and Hardy. I knew Stan and Ollie were famous, but I didn't expect them to be that well known in an Italian brothel. I was mistaken. The two girls were clearly upset by the inference. However, Madame waved away their protestations and asked if they were the two we would like to have as our "artistes." What a laugh, "artistes." We said they were fine, and away they went. The others, left, showing some displeasure at not being chosen, probably wishing they had looked more like Laurel and Hardy.

We were asked to follow Madame through the curtains at the end of the lounge. There we encountered a panel decor. She pushed against it, and we entered a small rotunda. It was like a gazebo. Eight huge mirrors framed an octagonal room, topped by a mirrored dome. Around the room were small stools covered in velvet. In the center was a very low double bed, its headrest decorated with cherubs, who were doing all sorts of strange things besides blowing trumpets.

I started to get claustrophobic when Madame closed the mirrored panel. Our twosome came in from behind another, stark naked, not even wearing a smile. Without as much as a "Hi, guys," they got on the bed and started with position number one—that one I already knew. After a few gyrations, they started to position themselves for the next. They were getting rather overheated and worked up, which was more than I was. After a few minutes, and only two positions accomplished out of the sixty-two shown on the villa walls, I realized we would miss the ship. I mentioned this fact to the boys, but they didn't seem interested.

I was becoming bored and rather sickened by the whole farce—not so Bob and Tommy. They were getting as worked up as the girls. The "artistes" decided it was time to strike. They first chose me, but I backed off, pointing to Bob and Tommy. They seemed to be ready for any position. leaving me, the girls went over to Tommy and started to undress him from the bottom up. I thought they were after the obvious, but I was wrong. They were after his wallet first.

Looking on, I joking said, "Make sure they give you a receipt."

The girls were getting rough, and I was getting scared. I got up and looked for a way out. There were no handles on the mirrored panels. I started to push at them, looking for spring locks to release us from this passion palace. There didn't seem to be any. But Stan did not want us to leave and began pulling at my trousers. Meanwhile, any feelings Bob and Tommy might have had to procreate had literally wilted away. Tommy, who had moved onto the bed, had now fallen off and was wrestling with Ollie, the large blonde, who was trying to get his wallet. It was a circus.

I decided there was only one course of action to take. Being very British, and always in full control during a crisis, I screamed out at the top of my voice, "Get us out of this bloody place!"

My cries were immediately answered as the mirrored panel in front of me opened, my reflection being replaced with a much larger man than any I had previously encountered. He pushed past me and grabbed Tommy and blonde Ollie, she still grappling with his trousers.

I decided to leave and, dashing out of the door, went straight into the curtains. I managed to extricate myself, only to find that I was near the bar. I felt like a drink, but common sense prevailed as I dashed to the stairs.

Standing at the top was our friend, the gentleman who had first greeted us. He didn't look so friendly now. He started to move toward me, as I took off in a flying tackle. Unfortunately, I started my attack a little too early. He saw me coming and sidestepped. The stairs were what I had to tackle now, as I bounced headlong down them. Fortunately, they were carpeted, and I knew how to fall. This did not stop me from getting bruised. The adrenaline was flowing, so I felt no pain at the time. I regained my footing and kept going. Was the taxi still there? I prayed it was.

As I reached the bottom of the staircase, the little old lady jumped in front of me with her palm outstretched. This was not the time for gratuities. I pushed past her and into the alleyway. Sure enough, leaning against the car was our driver. The engine was not running, but mine was. "Get the bloody thing started," I yelled.

With that, I turned around to see if Tommy and Bob had made it. Bob came puffing and blowing down the stairs. "They've got Tommy," he said. I started back up the stairs, as Tommy, in full flight, was coming down. We ran out to the alleyway and jumped into the car.

"How did you manage to get away?" I asked.

"I gave them my wallet," he said.

"What do you mean, your wallet? You left yours on the ship!"

Tommy looked at me in shock and dismay. "Oh, my God, it was yours."

My bruises started to hurt, as I turned to my mates and said, "Another fine mess you've got me into!"

This time we all laughed, including the driver.

We never did get to see all the positions those girls were going to show us. But we did learn one position never to get ourselves into if ever we found ourselves in Napoli again.

*   *   *

We sailed late that evening and made our way across the Mediterranean to our next port, Algiers. This was the one I had really been looking forward to. I was going to experience so many new things—a different culture, architecture, religion, and terrain.

We entered Algiers harbor at 7:30 A.M. on a clear, bright, sunny morning. The skyline of the city was already starting to shimmer in the early morning sunshine. It was going to be a hot day in more ways than one. As we came alongside the dock, the cries of the vendors selling their wares were blending with the calls of command from the Algerian pilot, as he docked the ship. The dock market stalls were full of colorful items: blankets, stuffed camels, and many items made of brass that reflected their presence in the sunlight.

I remember Kate had looked particularly beautiful that morning. She was wearing a white silk dress and a full-brimmed white hat she had bought in Naples. All four of us were looking smart and were eager to get off the ship. Just the thought of seeing the Casbah and the surrounding desert filled us with excitement.

We eventually made our way down the gangway and were met by a good-looking gentleman, holding a card with my name on it. Once again, the chief purser had done us proud. He had chosen this fine man to be our driver and guide for the day. The driver's name was Naki, and he spoke perfect English. We drove out of the dock gates and made our way through the town center for coffee at the King George V Hotel. Arriving at this elegant piece of architecture, we made our way onto the terrace, where we could see the Casbah, our next port of call. As we enjoyed our coffee, Naki told us of the civil unrest in the country, for Algeria, at that time, was trying to gain its independence from France. He said that if we were to go into the Casbah, we must keep close together and not stray off by ourselves. Because of the situation, he was apprehensive about our attractive girlfriends. Good-looking, single women had been known to disappear in this quarter of town. In view of Naki's comments, we thought it best if they stayed in the car. But they insisted on coming with us.

The Casbah lay down in a gully, and steps wound down into its interior through narrow streets. The buildings, all painted white to reflect the sun, were mainly small shops and quaint dwellings. All this, with the cries of the vendors, accompanied by strains of Arabic music, created an unimagined aura of timeless explorations, exotic tales, and indelible images of intrigue and wonder.

Children continually circled us with their hands outstretched and their faces bearing the solemn look of misery practiced by beggars the world over. However, these children were well-dressed and far from starving. There were other children, not begging, who seemed more interested in knowing what was going on behind certain iron fret screens. These others were gathered in a small group with their faces pressed against the screens, looking and listening to the music coming from within. Naki told us they were not really listening to the music but trying to see some of the action. Evidently, behind the screens, there were brothels, very much a part of the life in the Casbah.

Expecting to see Humphrey Bogart any second, we continued farther down the street. Naki seemed to sense something and suggested that we make our way back to the car. As we turned to walk back, a scuffle broke out above us on the steps. Naki pulled us into a doorway, as a small crowd of Arabs came rushing by and seized a young man, throwing him to the ground. They started to beat and kick him down the steps. Shocked by the sight, we quickly made our way back up the steps to the entrance.

We got into the car, hot, bothered, and a little shaken. Naki apologized for the incident, though, obviously, it was no fault of his. He was, like all good guides, eager to have us see his country and people at their best and upset when things happened to offend the visitor. We all agreed that a good stiff drink was in order, and Naki suggested the bar at the Sheraton Hotel. As we entered the main square, we found it full of tanks and armored cars. French soldiers were stationed outside the main buildings, and there was a distinct feeling of crisis. I suggested to Naki he ask one of the soldiers what was going on, but he did not seem keen on the idea.

We found the Sheraton surrounded by more soldiers, who asked to see our identification. They would not allow Naki to accompany us into the hotel. So, reluctantly, Naki returned to the car park.

The hotel bar was comfortable and was a peaceful haven after our experiences of the morning. We took our seats at the bar, attended by the most qualified news source to be found anywhere in the world, a barman. As he poured us four large gin and tonics, we asked him what was going on in the city. That morning, he told us, there had been a massacre in the town of Ain Abid, several miles along the coast. All the victims had been Europeans. The National Liberation Front was responsible, and the authorities in Algiers were very much on the alert. We decided on a quick lunch and ordered sandwiches, so as not to keep Naki waiting too long.

We returned to the car park and asked Naki, in view of the situation, to return us to the ship. We drove back through the city and arrived safe and sound at the dock gates. This area was also heavily guarded with tanks and armored vehicles, and French soldiers were operating a very tight security check here as well. Again, Naki was not allowed to accompany us onto the docks. So, after thanking him with a handsome tip, we said our farewells and walked back to the ship.

The dock was full of passengers who were keeping the stall holders busy. Most passengers had come back to the ship because of the situation. This made for big business on the dock. Cruise ships add a tremendous amount to a port's economy. Figures may vary, but, on docking, it is said that a port can look at a minimum of one hundred dollars per passenger, and that does not include the crew. Hong Kong, however, puts this figure at more than a thousand dollars per passenger. I added to the Algerian economy by buying a brass coal bucket, which stands by my fireplace to this day.

That evening we sailed for the Strait of Gibraltar, the gateway to the Atlantic. After dinner, Kate and I went on deck to see the famous rock as we sailed by. For centuries, it has stood as a sentry to the famous strait. The lights of Gibraltar flickered in recognition as we left the blue of the Mediterranean for the grey of the Atlantic.

After an uneventful sailing along the coast of Spain and Portugal, we turned into the estuary of the Tagus River. This is the main artery to the great city of Lisbon. The early morning arrival took us past the fine architecture of the outlying suburbs, the magnificent buildings of earlier centuries, and the famous statue of Peter the Navigator, its many figures flanking the central figure of the explorer. On the starboard side, the looming statue of Christ stands beside the Salazar Bridge, which spans the river.

Passing under the great steel girders, we moved toward our dock, where many people were gathered to greet the ship. It was the ship's first call, and, as with all the other ports, special celebrations had been arranged. Eventually, we docked in front of an impressive passenger terminal and, very soon, were making our way down the gangway. Outside the terminal, I walked over to the best-looking taxi and stood beside it, calling to its owner. So often you haggle with a driver; then, on agreeing, you wind up in the biggest load of rubbish on four wheels. By staking out the car first, one can be assured of at least a comfortable ride, if the price is right. (It was the chief purser who taught me this one!)

Fortunately, the driver spoke reasonably good English, and after getting the price sorted out, we made our way into the center of Lisbon for a coffee at one of the elegant cafés that border the Figueria Square. Since this was our last port, we decided to visit some of the elegant shops for which Lisbon is famous. After spending more than I could afford on an expensive pair of shoes, we returned to the car and made our way west out of the city to Cascais, a fishing port near the mouth of the Tagus estuary, which we had passed on our way in. We were told it was famous for its fish restaurants. We chose a restaurant where you could select a fish or lobster directly out of the tank. Our seafood meal was excellent, and I rate it as one of the finest I have ever had.

After this feast fit for a king, we drove back along the coast to Estoril, the playground of the rich in Portugal. Here are excellent beaches and cafés, also an elegant casino in which we gambled a few escudos. We decided to drive back to the ship and relax by the pool before cocktails and dinner on board. After dinner, the four of us took a walk off the ship along the dock road. Here, we found a small café. After enjoying a brandy, we noticed they were selling cases of Portuguese sparkling wine for a ridiculously low price. We decided then and there to have a sail-away party and bought three cases.

Arriving back on board, we got hold of friends we had made through the cruise and invited them up to the aft deck at sailing time. It was a great scene for a deck party. The statue of Christ stood behind us, his face lit up with the arc lights from beneath. The lights of Lisbon reflected against a cloudy sky, forming a veritable blanket of light over the whole city. Our ship enhanced the scene, dressed overall with a string of lights from stem to stern. This all created a wonderful atmosphere for our midnight sailing. The sound of the windlass turning as it pulled in our mooring ropes mingled with the sound of traffic from the bridge as it ran over the steel roadway. This fanfare of sound heralded our departure. Slowly, the *Southern Cross* moved away from the dock to make its way under the bridge and down the estuary. The ship's whistle gave a blast of farewell and, for us, the perfect signal to pop the first cork of our sparkling wine, the first of thirty-six. . . .

We had gone no more than twenty yards from the dock when a taxi screamed to a halt. From it leapt a passenger. We all recognized her as she ran from the cab to the edge of the dock. Her name was Bonnie, and she hailed from Dundee in Scotland. She was hardly a frail lass, to say the least. Her attentions during the cruise had been directed toward the bos'n, who was Scottish.

Bonnie started to appeal to the captain, in no uncertain

terms, to return the ship to the dock. This was not going to happen, the captain having more important things to deal with at the time. One of our agents on the dock quickly went over and calmed her down. An officer standing with us said the agent would put her on the pilot boat bringing her to our ship.

As the *Southern Cross* continued up the river, our party grew bigger as more friends joined us. Half an hour had gone by when one of our party sighted the pilot boat. On it, we could see Bonnie's ample figure as she waved like crazy. More passengers came from within the ship to greet her. The pilot boat came alongside, and a rope ladder was dropped from the ship. It was obvious from the start that Bonnie had no intention of climbing up the daunting rope ladder. Her piteous protestations rang out in the night air, loud and clear. She pushed the pilot boat seaman away, as her shouts of refusal in colorful Scottish wafted upwards to the many passengers lining the rails.

The situation seemed hopeless. Then, like a knight in shining dungarees, the bos'n was seen climbing down the rope ladder. A cheer went up from the passengers as he reached the deck of the pilot boat and stood beside his damsel in distress. Resting his hands gently on Bonnie's shoulders and looking straight into her eyes, he talked to her in a calm and caring manner. A few moments later, she started slowly up the rope ladder with him close behind.

Halfway up, it all came to a halt. She lost her nerve, her harrowing predicament now hitting home.

A sailor appeared at the top of the rope ladder and started down. He offered his hand to help pull her up. She rejected it. Now desperate, the bos'n simply pushed rudely upwards in an area he had recently treated with more respect. With all the shoving and pulling, they eventually managed to get her to the top of the ladder. Tearful and exhausted, she was pulled onto the ship. Rousing cheers broke out in appreciation of the efforts made by all concerned.

I asked one of our party to go down and see if Bonnie would like to join the party. He returned to say he could not find her. I think she wanted to thank the bos'n in a way only a grateful Scottish maiden would know how.

Oblivious to Bonnie's humiliation, our party went on until the wee small hours, the empty bottles bouncing in the wake of the ship, as one by one they were tossed overboard. They held no message, save their presence telling of a great party given by four very happy cruisers, a fitting finale for a cruise packed with excitement and fun. I knew now that cruising was the only way to go. Little did I know then how far.

The last two days at sea were filled with lots of laughs and fun. The Bay of Biscay, usually an unpredictable stretch of water, was as calm as a mill pond. I remember playing and losing in the deck quoits finals, but my prize for that cruise was Kate.

The last morning dawned to find the *Southern Cross* sailing up the English Channel. The bright sunshine of the day before had gone and was replaced by dense fog and the sounds of the ship's horn. We passed the Isle of Wight, unable to see the famous outcrops of rock called the Needles. The fog started lifting, as we made our way up Southampton water to pier 104.

Eventually, we docked and, as we waited for clearance, the Royal Marines band played for us on the pier. It was a nice touch and one I have never forgotten. Finally, the ship was cleared, and the four of us made our way down the gangway for the last time. Kate lived many miles from me and was going home by train. I would ring her that evening to make a date for later that week. I was driving home to London. After going through customs, we picked up our luggage and made our way to the outer area and the train platform. I turned to Kate, and her smiling lips joined with mine as we kissed good-bye. As she boarded the train, which had been waiting in the terminal, the whistle heralded its departure. We both waved until the train reached a bend and disappeared out of sight.

As I walked away from the platform, the ship's resonant whistle sounded as if to attract my attention. I turned and looked at the *Southern Cross*. Little did I know then that my life was about to change. On this ship, I had fallen in love, not only with a girl but with ships, with cruising, and with the sea.

Selling motor cars was not a shipboard occupation. There had to be a way for me to earn a living on a cruise ship.

I phoned Kate that evening and arranged to meet her later in the week. I wanted her to meet my friends and my mum and dad. I picked her up at her apartment in London and drove the eleven miles to my home in Enfield. For the first time, I saw my father do a double take when he met her. She hit it off with both my parents.

I drove her back to London and, as dawn was breaking, kissed her good morning in the chill morning air and drove home. As I drove out of London, I felt a nothingness. Something had left me. I no longer felt the same about Kate. Looking back over our short time together, I could not remember one thing we had in common except the cruise. On reflection, our conversations had had no depth. Most of them had involved the ship and the places we had been enjoying together.

Then it struck me. I was a victim of a shipboard romance. Our relationship had been nurtured in an unreal environment. I realized the problem ahead of me. How was I going to be the one to tell her it was all off? I had no idea the relationship was solely based on a romantic experience. I had been seduced by the ship and the sea. On the other hand, mightn't she also be feeling the same and be relieved if I took the initiative and broke off the relationship? The captain of the *Southern Cross* knew the spell that the sea and the ships could spin around young couples, and around older ones, come to that.

The dread of having to tell Kate did not materialize. I phoned the next day, and she told me she was going on a modeling engagement in Scotland. She said she would ring when she got back. She didn't. I rang some days later only to be told that she was out for the evening and would ring me when she returned. I never received the call. I was off the hook!

I learned a lot from that relationship with Kate. I worry when I see passengers who think they're having a serious affair on board, and I wonder if they are expecting it to be the same once their feet hit terra firma. Meeting each other in your own home environment can create quite a different picture. It's the lonely single person looking for a serious relationship who worries me most. For those working on board, it is different. The glamour soon wears off when you live at sea. It is not the same for those of us who are involved in the day-to-day operation of a cruise ship. They who choose to live together on a ship have the opportunity to see each other in all sorts of stressful or mundane situations. This is not a bad basis for a long and a successful relationship.

Barbara and I worked closely on board for three years before we married. Since then, as man and wife, we have lived and worked happily ever since. I suppose we can be considered experts on "love on the love boats."

A year later, Derek Stocking, a sales manager and my boss at the time, said something strange to me. My enthusiasm for cruising had gotten to him, and he and his wife had gone on a cruise to the Canary Islands in the Atlantic. On his return, he called me into his office and thanked me for introducing him to cruising. "Derek," he said, "I don't want you to think I am not happy with your work, but, whilst on the cruise, I discovered the perfect job for you."

"Really, what is it? I asked inquisitively.

"A cruise director," he replied.

It took me nineteen years to become one. But, let's face it, that man sure had foresight.

III

Cruise Director's Chronicles

Introduction

My father was born in London in 1898 and my mother in Scotland six years later. In 1975, when I decided to go to sea, they were living in a town called Ware. It lies some twenty-two miles north of London in the county of Hertfordshire. Their home was a small bungalow, where they lived a quiet life. I was their only child. Our relationship had always been close, and I involved them with nearly everything in which I was associated. It was quite a blow for them when, after my first marriage broke up, I decided to leave England and travel the world. However, I promised I would write regularly, and I did. It became a pleasant duty to let them know where I was, and I was happy to do anything that might lighten their comparatively dull lives.

Over the years, I took them on three cruises. The first, which celebrated their fiftieth wedding anniversary, was a cruise to Norway and coincided with the fiftieth anniversary of the death of Edvard Grieg, Norway's greatest composer. On our arrival in Bergen, the Norwegians proclaimed the fact with banners on which were displayed the numeral 50 writ large. My mother thought I had arranged the welcome banners for them, until I told them of the coincidence.

My father, who had always been a home lover, was a pain when it came to going away. He liked to ride his bicycle and watch his cricket from the boundary fence. Even though I had made him a member of the cricket club for him to enjoy the comfort of the pavilion, he preferred (when I was not there) to stay outside, sitting on his bike with the "poor people." My father was a very shy man, something I did not realize until I was much older. However, that evening, when I said proudly, "I'm taking you on a cruise to Norway for your fiftieth anniversary," my mother started to cry, but my dad, unimpressed, started to make all sorts of excuses for not going.

"I haven't got the right clothes, he whined.

"I'll buy you some," I said.

"I only like your mother's cooking. I can't deal with all that fancy food."

"Dad, they serve eggs and bacon, steak and chips, all the things you like. You'll love the food," I told him.

"And what am I going to do all day? I'll be bored stiff, and I'll miss the exercise on my bike."

"Darn your bike," my mother said. "We're going, and that's that. Now, shut up and make a cup of tea."

When he'd returned with the tea and biscuits, Dad still kept on about being bored.

"Don't you ever read all the programs I send you?" I asked. "There are dozens of activities. Most of my passengers need a holiday to recover from a cruise with me."

The great day arrived when they flew to Copenhagen to pick up the *Royal Viking Star*. Everybody made a fuss over them, and they had the time of their lives. My father never complained of being bored, and, to top it off, he loved the food.

I was at home when Dad passed away, but when told my mother was dying, I was in the Caribbean. Unfortunately, as I boarded the plane in San Juan, she died. Mother had decided to return to Scotland after sixty-three years in England and had finished her days in a "home for retired gentlefolk," not all that far from the village where she was born. I now had that sad and emotional duty of getting her clothes and belongings out of her room.

All that remained after eighty-seven years of her life was in that little room. The walls held so many photos of our happy times together. Memories flooded back as I took each photograph down and put it away. Under her bed, I found her suitcase. In it, to my amazement, I found every postcard and letter I had ever written. I sat down on her little bed and started to relive my life through those letters. People, places, events, and experiences came alive again. I read for a long time, and, as I put down the last letter, my eyes filled with tears. I realized that that was the last one I would ever write to my parents.

Reading the postcards evoked memories of adventures I had shared with them over the years, and I offer some of these memories to the gentle reader.

Up from the Deep

I have always been a sea watcher looking at the waters of the Gulf of Alaska. Only minutes ago I watched a humpback whale rise up in farewell, its fluke waved above the surface before it sank beneath the rippling sea to continue its journey to its feeding grounds. But whales are not all I have sighted from the promenade deck of a cruise ship. Three stories come to mind of things coming up from the deep.

There have been fascinating stories since time immemorial of the possibly mythic relationship between mankind and creatures of the deep. Stories recur throughout many cultures of the hero riding the dolphin, of Jonah and the whale, and so on. Even in our day, just hours after the tragedy of the *Challenger* explosion and the loss of the seven astronauts over the Atlantic Ocean, there was the authenticated and deeply moving story of seven dolphins rising up from the sea in circular formation and turning seven times in the water, as if in homage to the fallen, before submerging and disappearing from view into the ocean.

In 1981, I was present at another awesome incident that occurred in the North Atlantic off the coast of Spain, another tribute to drowned heroes.

We were sailing from the Mediterranean to Lisbon and had stopped for a morning in Gibraltar. I had gone to the cemetery where some of the sailors lay who had fought in the battle of Trafalgar. I knew we would be passing the historic cape in the afternoon and decided to hold a short service as we sailed past in memory of those who had died in the battle. On my way back to the ship, I bought a wreath to cast off the ship.

We sailed at lunchtime, and, after I had welcomed the returning passengers, I spoke to the captain about my idea. He liked it and said he would slow down the ship as we passed the cape. He then informed the navigator of the plan.

When I returned to my cabin, I decided it might be appropriate to describe the battle, using the points on the coastline as reference. Fortunately, we had the *Encyclopaedia Britannica* on board, so I studied the battle for an hour to get my facts right. At approximately 4:00 P.M., I went to the bridge with my notes and the wreath.

I went to the loudspeaker and began to set the scene for the passengers. The weather was perfect, and the captain helped me by sailing nearer the shore, so it was fairly easy to see the landmarks. After doing my best to bring the battle between Admirals Nelson and Villeneuve alive, I played a recording of the sailors' hymn, "Eternal Father, Strong to Save." As the hymn drew to a close, the captain and I took the wreath to the wing of the bridge and cast it on the waters. The ship's whistle sounded, and I concluded the ceremony by saying, "We now leave this graveyard of the Battle of Trafalgar. May these brave men always rest in peace."

Suddenly, beside the wreath, a monstrous object rose up from the surging waters. It was at least forty feet in length. Long tentacles briefly came above the water, as it brushed beside the wreath, and then slowly glided back under the waves.

It was a weird experience, and for a moment we were speechless. "What is it?" we kept asking ourselves. Eventually, we decided it could only be one thing: we had all seen our first giant squid. But this one was special. It was the guardian of the sunken ships and of the fallen of the Battle of Trafalgar.

In 1979, we were sailing across the Pacific from Los Angeles to the Polynesian Islands, when something just as spectacular occurred.

From Los Angeles the cruise takes nine days to reach the beautiful island of Bora Bora, our first destination. On the sixth day out, we crossed the equator. For hundreds of years, seafarers have held initiation ceremonies for those who are crossing the line for the first time. Tradition demands the convening of a mock court for Neptune and his queen. The court is conducted by those who have crossed before—they're called "shellbacks." In the ceremony, the initiates, called "pollywogs, "are summoned to the court, and the shellbacks have the job of getting them there.

In my early days at sea, I saw some rowdy and overenthusiastic ceremonies, with people chased all over the ship, then waylaid and rudely escorted to the court. Sometimes, there were accidents that resulted in bruises and broken bones. So when I became cruise director, I followed my friend Pat Buckle's script and performed the trial as a show instead. This put an end to the dangerous horseplay and got the maximum amount of fun without mishaps.

On one occasion, as was usually the case, the ship was decorated with flags as we approached the equator. The area around the pool was set up with thrones for Neptune and his queen, and the selected pollywogs were led into the area by a motley band of musicians, pirates, and a mock surgeon and his nurses. The pollywogs—who ultimately would be sentenced for various comic crimes, operated on, then doused with ketchup and spaghetti and tossed in the pool—were penned in a "jail" on the opposite side from the musicians, guarded by pirates. I acted as the prosecutor, the master of ceremonies actually, and the captain was on hand to greet Neptune personally. Neptune (wearing a crown and a long beard, and carrying a scepter and trident) and his queen (played by a particularly unlovely guy in drag) were lurking in the lower afterdeck so that they would seem to make their appearance from the deep. Neptune and I were well coordinated, so that, as I concluded my opening remarks, which were in rhyme, he and his lady would appear suddenly at the pool.

The band played a fanfare, and I read a proclamation to herald the arrival of Neptune and his court. I launched into the last stanza;

> And now let's welcome Neptune,
> Who's woken from his sleep,
> Surrounded by his noble court,
> And his creatures from the deep.

At this moment, when Neptune appeared by the pool, a majestic slob, the sea began to stir. Whales surfaced on the starboard side, and all around us the ocean was full of porpoises, at least a hundred of them. We all gasped at the sight, the passengers all started laughing and cheering, and Neptune tripped on his cloak. As he lunged forward, off balance, his scepter and trident sailed into the pool. The rest of his court tried to remain dignified and stately, but, with his efforts to retrieve his lost symbols of power, he again lost his balance and disappeared into the pool.

For a full five minutes, we watched enthralled at this double spectacle, the creatures of deep performing their water ballet and the poor king his. When the creatures finally left us beneath the waves, I surveyed the sodden Neptune, his court, and the passengers.

Then, with a voice full of dignity, I said, "Your Majesty, ladies and gentlemen, as you are traveling the Royal Viking Line, we have naturally provided nothing but the best."

Over the years, I have sailed around South America several times. Somehow mysterious things always seem to happen on these cruises. I know of passengers who go time and time again, purely out of fascination with what could happen next. In 1984, we suddenly replaced the world cruise with an unusual tour of South America. Regular passengers of the Royal Viking Line were perplexed by this, but many came out of loyalty and would not sail with any other line. It was not a good cruise. Having to miss out on many important excursions, as well as having to contend with constant bad weather and illness, made crew and passengers alike jumpy and uneasy.

With all the other problems, there was the ominous rumor of imminent war between Chile and Argentina. In Valparaiso, we had picked up nervous Chilean pilots who would take us through the distant inland waterways of their country. They would be leaving us in the Strait of Magellan right at the Argentine border. By now, what had begun as unwelcome rumors when we left Valparaiso had escalated to the point of panic amongst the passengers. They started to petition the captain for an immediate return to Valparaiso.

The captain had no choice but to send a telex to the president of the Royal Viking Line requesting that he contact the U.S. State Department to ascertain the real situation between the two countries. The reply came back a few hours later, stating that the rumor seemed completely unfounded.

The captain felt it would be best if I made the announcement from the bridge on the emergency system. We were now entering the Strait of Magellan, and naturally many passengers were on deck. I arrived on the bridge to find the Chilean pilots seemingly in a more relaxed state of mind. Though I usually make these announcements off the "top of my head," this time I decided to read from written notes.

"Ladies and Gentlemen," I said, noting that the passengers were paying rapt attention, "we have just received the following telex from the head office in San Francisco. At the request of the master of the *Royal Viking Sky*, we have contacted the State Department in Washington to determine whether a state of emergency exists between Chile and Argentina. The State Department assures us that no such situation exists between these two countries. Therefore, we have no reason to be concerned about our safety in these waters."

But as I spoke these last words, a sleek black form swiftly emerged from the depths of the sea within a few hundred yards of us on the port side, in full view of the passengers. I could hear their shrieks as the water cascaded off this towering form's hull. Thunderstruck, we were faced with the realization that this was actually a submarine! Astonished myself, I said, "Oh, shit!" With the quick thinking they pay me for, I also had the sense to turn off the mike before I said it.

The captain, who was standing beside me, looked at me coolly. "Now what are you going to say?" he asked me.

I switched the mike back on and, trying to show calm, said, in a matter-of-fact voice, "Well, we appear to have a submarine escorting us at this time. Let's have a word with its captain and find out with whom we have the *pleasure* of sailing this famous strait."

The chief officer called up the sub on the radio, while I put the call onto the public-address system so the passengers would be privy to the conversation. To our collective amazement, a very British voice answered, "This is Commander Anderson of the Royal Navy."

I took the radio mike. "May I ask what a British submarine is doing in this neck of the woods?" I managed to ask politely.

"British no longer," he replied. "It has been purchased by the Chilean navy. At present, we are on a training cruise, showing the Chilean officers and crew the ropes."

Commander Anderson proceeded to ask about the number of passengers we were carrying and where we were headed. I gave him the information and told him of the war rumor and of his disconcerting timing.

"Oh, dear," he said, "I hope we didn't give you all too much of a scare."

With that, we said our farewells, and he left us to ponder this melodramatic finale to a bleak tour, aware of our vulnerability against monsters, mythic and modern, and the unknown. The commander continued his cruise under the water and we ours on top of it.

Collectors' Items

In past years, many items around the ship would have the logo of the line imprinted on them. These would be an inevitable target for souvenir hunters. The *Queen Mary,* for instance, lost thousands of ashtrays on her first voyage. Hotels and ships have always calculated a loss of these items within their budgets, but sometimes the number of items taken goes way over the estimate. Nowadays, only cruise shops sell logo items. A story comes to mind involving not only the "collecting bug," but also a drinking problem.

In 1989, we were sailing out of Vancouver for our Alaska cruising season. That year saw the hundredth anniversary of the impressive Vancouver Hotel. In the foyer was an excellent display of the hotel through the years. This was supported by many fine photographs and memorabilia. Eighty percent of the items had been sent by guests, who, over the years, had taken away a little "memory" of their visit. The Vancouver had advertised in all the top newspapers around the world for items "borrowed" from the hotel. They had also offered to return them to their new owners when the exhibition had finished.

While enjoying looking at the Victorian bedroom, the elegant table setup, and all the fascinating bric-a-brac, my mind went back a few years earlier to a dock on the West Coast.

We had just returned from Alaska, and some five hundred passengers had departed through the customs area. In front of the customs officer was a lady in a wheelchair. Standing behind her was her companion. Please do not feel too sorry for the lady in the wheelchair. Her need of the vehicle, borrowed from our hospital, did not arise from reasons of a serious nature. At this particular time, her ability to walk was restricted by her addiction to spirits, which had departed from the bottle into her ample frame.

Drinking to excess was all part of a way of life in cruising years ago. People are more health-conscious nowadays and quench their thirst with soft drinks—not so this couple.

The weather was poor at the start of the cruise, and by nighttime, it had become very rough. Many passengers stayed in their cabins and "laid low."

Two maiden ladies of indeterminate age were doing

their level best to ward off seasickness with a remedy that does not get a lot of support from the medical profession. The two bottles of gin they had brought with them were rolling lazily across the floor of their cabin when the stewardess came in the next morning. After a very rocky night, the cabin was in a terrible state, and the bathroom was even worse. The two ladies were fast asleep, so she decided to clean up around them. The beds could wait till later. The stewardess reported the situation to the housekeeper and went to lunch.

The housekeeper called on the two occupants after lunch to see how they were getting along. The cabin was empty, and so she made the beds herself. At 2:30 that afternoon, the nurse was called to the bar. One of the ladies had fallen from her stool at the bar. Upon examination, she was found to have no broken bones. People who are inebriated have a way of falling in a nice relaxed state that seems to ward off breakages. The nurse took the fallen lady to her cabin just as the housekeeper was leaving. At the same time, the other lady was making her way along the corridor very much the worse for wear, looking through squinting eyes at the numbers on the cabin doors. The nurse and the housekeeper helped both ladies get inside their cabin and suggested they go to bed. The hotel manager was informed.

That evening, the two women appeared late for dinner (the ship had only one sitting). They were not in a good mood when they found they were seated at a table for eight. Needless to say, this arrangement did not last long, as the others at the table asked to be moved for the next meal on the very next day.

The following morning the stewardess decided to leave their cabin until last. No sign was on the door, and at 10:00 A.M. she knocked. No reply. She decided to enter. In front of her was a repeat performance of the night before. This time, the weather could not be blamed. The hotel manager was called, and later that day, the two ladies met him. They were warned that they would be asked to leave the ship if they did not reduce their drinking.

That evening they were given a table for two. The wine flowed, and their voices were raised to such an extent that the other passengers complained. A decision was made to serve them their meals in their cabin for the rest of the voyage. There they boozed, ate little, and slept for the rest of the cruise.

The stewardess was now reporting the loss of silver and other items from their cabin. The mohair blanket had gone, plus pillow slips, etc., etc. The hotel manager decided to let it ride for the time being.

The only time the two ladies left the ship was to visit our last port of call, Victoria, the capital of British Columbia. They apparently needed to do some shopping. I watched them come back up the gangway with two large new suitcases!

Eventually, we arrived at our port of debarkation. All passengers had been asked to vacate their cabins by 8:00 A.M. The stewardess reported that our two friends were still in bed. They were both very drunk, one more than the other. They had apparently been sober enough to put their bags out the previous evening. The doctor and the hotel manager were called; I was asked to find the luggage and make sure it was placed by the gangway for customs.

I went to see the customs officers and told them the situation. They would make a full inspection of the luggage when the two ladies eventually came down. To minimize any embarrassment, the inspection was done after most of the other passengers had left. We took the ladies to their luggage for identification and then to the customs table. The first suitcase of the five produced nothing, but the other four held enough to start a bed and breakfast. I kept a list of the items customs found:

    31 pieces of table silver
    12 plates, all with the "RVL" logo
    11 pillow cases
     9 pieces of glassware
     2 mohair blankets
    15 table napkins
     9 small coffee saucers
    10 coffee cups
     9 ashtrays, 2 of them large cut glass
    20 miscellaneous items from the gift shop

To top it all off, there was even a toilet brush!

After these two passengers had been made to feel very guilty and told they would be fined five hundred dollars, the hotel manager asked the officer to waive any fine or action. I escorted them to a limousine, where their chauffeur had been patiently waiting. I helped them into the car and took back our wheelchair. As I said good-bye, the elder one took my hand and said, "Thank you, captain, for a safe trip, and I hope we meet again."

Had I known then what I know now, I would have suggested that they take their next vacation at the Vancouver Hotel, where management seems more tolerant of "borrowed" items.

Just a Matter of Time

Many of you have experienced jet lag. At sea, we do not have that problem in quite the same way. Sailing across time zones is dealt with at much slower speeds, one day at a time. This makes the transition much easier on the mind and body. However, when you are sailing around the world and visiting many different countries, time changes are not always easy to calculate. Because your ship is sailing in a westerly or easterly direction, you clearly have to put your clock either back or forward one hour. But there's a catch.

Some countries make time changes they do not inform others about. It is not unusual for one province within a country to have a different time zone from another province quite nearby. It can get rather confusing.

On one cruise around South America, we got so mixed up, passengers were calling out to passing fishing boats to find the correct hour. The passengers would start to laugh whenever I walked on the stage after the show. I would say, "Well, ladies and gentlemen, I have no idea what time it is. Suffice it to say, the buffet will open in half an hour." It got laughs from the Amazon to Valparaiso, Chile. On one occasion, we called the international telephone operator for the time, and she got it wrong. We decided at one port to keep the passengers on ship's time. This meant all passengers and crew synchronized their watches with the ship's clocks, not the time on the Town Hall clock on shore, which had never been right since Adam was a boy. It worked out fine, and nobody missed the ship.

On the 1978 world cruise, we had a situation that can only be described as unique and a cruise director's nightmare. We sailed from Fort Lauderdale through the Panama Canal to Los Angeles. From there, we made our way to the South Seas and Australia; then we continued on to Bali, Singapore, and India. The last leg home took us through the Suez Canal, stopping at Port Said, Alexandria, Malta, and Malaga. After Malaga, we sailed to Tangier, before crossing the Atlantic via Madeira to New York.

We were now seventy-five days into the ninety-day

cruise. Everything had been going well, but things were about to change. We arrived at the Tangier pilot station in plenty of time to pick the pilot up at 7:00 A.M. He would take us into our dock, and the gangway would be down by 8:00 A.M. I was on the bridge early to pay my respects to the captain and his officers.

It was a bright, clear morning as we waited for signs of the pilot boat coming from the harbor. The familiar Arabian architecture of Tangier was already starting to shimmer from the heat of the early morning sun. After the usual morning pleasantries, I said to the captain, "No sign of the pilot yet, Captain?"

"No, but we're early," he replied.

I looked at my watch which showed it to be 7:30 A.M.

I thought he was supposed to be here at seven," I said.

"That's right," the captain replied.

"Well, it's seven-thirty on my watch," I stated.

"Derek," he said, "the clocks went back one hour last night."

I froze, as I realized I had forgotten to put it in the program. The passengers and crew had all gotten up one hour late, except, of course, for the bridge. I phoned the hotel manager and told him the problem. He was not pleased. We had all missed it on our cruise plan given to us by the navigator at the beginning of the cruise.

We decided not to tell the passengers for the time being until the pilot arrived. The problem was now to contact the agent and tour operator to get things going more quickly than they had planned. We called the agent first—no reply. The same thing occurred with the tour operator and the pilot station. Usually, the port agents, pilots, and officials are around early when a ship is coming in, especially a passenger vessel.

While we were talking, I picked up the binoculars and

looked around the town and the harbor. Here it was just after 7:00 A.M. in a big city, and there was no sign of life anywhere, not even a dog or an early riser. There was a stillness that was eerie in that early morning sunshine. On closer inspection, I saw people lying on the pavements, against the walls of buildings, in doorways, and by the harbor wall. They were lying unnaturally still. I turned to the captain beside me and said, "Look at the streets, Captain. I think we have a problem." He took the binoculars and scanned the town slowly.

After taking the glasses away from his face, he looked at me and said just one word, with feeling, "Jesus!"

No wonder we could not raise anybody. It would appear there had been an insurrection. The captain ordered the chief officer to keep on emergency channel 16 to get some response from the shore. He told the radio officer to keep listening to the World Service of the BBC, or to Voice of America. Maybe he could pick up some news about Tangier. The captain decided to phone the president of the company at his home in San Francisco. Then he could contact the State Department in Washington to find out what problems there might be in Tangier.

By now, it was nearly 7:30 A.M., and the passengers had to be wondering why we were still outside the harbor. I decided to get on the system and apologize for the delay, telling them only that we would let them know when the pilot was approaching the ship.

Making my way back to my office, the navigator called me into the chart room. He looked serious as he said, "I've dropped an awful brick."

"Join the club," I said.

"This is not funny," he replied. "I've just realized Tangier is on double summertime. The clocks should have gone back two hours last night, not one."

In all my years at sea, I have never known, excuse the

expression, such a cock-up. Now, we had a real problem on our hands. The passengers who ate breakfast at 7:00 A.M. were really eating it at 5:00 A.M.! If we went on Tangier time now, it would be hopeless. The tour buses on land were due at 8:30 A.M. their time, but that was now going to be 10:30 A.M. on our ship's time. As it was now only 7:30 A.M., the passengers were going to have to wait another three hours before they went on tour. By then, their tummies were going to tell them it was lunch hour! I have never been so embarrassed and upset. How on earth were we going to deal with such a ridiculous situation?

The captain was just putting the phone down from his call to San Francisco as I walked into his cabin. He looked up at me and said, "They don't have any information about the problem here."

"Well, captain," I replied, "I suggest you remain seated and prepare yourself for a shock. The navigator and I will probably be leaving here to live and play with the ships of the desert. All we ask is that the band play 'Now Is the Hour' as you cast us adrift. What we saw on the streets were homeless beggars. They are asleep because it is now only 5:30 A.M. Tangier is *two* hours behind us. They are on double summertime. I suggest we tell the passengers there is an outbreak of some terrible disease here; therefore, we are sailing on to Madeira. I never did like this place anyway."

He looked at me and shook his head. "Well, I wish you and the hotel manager luck in sorting this mess out," he said sternly. "In all my years at sea, I have never experienced anything like this. It makes us all look like idiots."

I left him putting his clock back another hour and his confidence in the navigator and me back ten years.

I called the hotel manager, who was extremely upset, to say the least. He quickly called a meeting of department heads. The chef, the maître d', and the others in the kitchen were going to have me for dinner. We met in the conference room, and after I had apologized on behalf of the navigator and myself, we got down to the business of working out all the changes that had to be made. The chef said he would prepare box lunches for those on tour or for anyone who wanted to take one. The galley would also prepare a full lunch buffet from 10:00 A.M. on. The tour times and other program alterations would be printed, distributed, and posted around the ship. I had already contacted my assistant and devised activities to keep passengers occupied until they could go ashore. Now the time had come when yours truly had to go on the PA system and tell the passengers of the mess we had gotten ourselves into.

When things untoward happen on a ship, I have always made it a policy to tell the facts as they are. I simply keep as close to the truth as possible, without embarrassing any particular member of the ship's company. Only when the situation is life threatening and there is a possibility of panic do I deviate from the truth.

In fact, on two occasions, I have been involved in a bomb scare on board. One of these occurred while we were in Australia. As we were leaving Sydney Harbor, the captain received a call from the Sydney police. They told him they had received a phone call from a person saying he had planted a bomb on our ship, the *Royal Viking Star*. The bomb was due to go off some time before midnight. The police asked us to continue out of the harbor and to anchor a mile outside the entrance.

After consulting with the captain, I told the passengers that the Sydney police had reason to believe a large consignment of drugs had been placed on board. I said the drug squad would be coming in half an hour and we would be grateful if the passengers would cooperate with them as requested. You can imagine what would have happened had

I told the truth. It was an anxious time for those of us who were privy to the real reason. It actually took four hours for the bomb squad to make sure the ship was "clean." Only after they left—incidentally, with four magnificent German shepherds that they had brought, specially trained to smell out explosives—did I tell the passengers the truth. They were relieved and grateful for the way the ship had dealt with the situation.

Well, my sunrise announcement was going to be different. I could not demean the navigator, so I decided to halve the blame and put some humor into the announcement. Everyone knew me by now and seemed to enjoy my sense of humor. It was sure going to be put to the test with this news. I cleared my throat, hit the button, and away I went.

"Ladies and Gentlemen, may I have your undivided attention for a very important announcement. Many of you are at this time under the impression it is 8:00 A.M. I am afraid you are wrong. It is only 6:00 A.M. in Tangier. You must be wondering how this can be. Well, half the fault is mine. Last night, I forgot to tell you to put your clocks back one hour. On arriving this morning at Tangier, the navigator and I found, to our horror, that Tangier is on double summertime. This raises one or two problems that, doubtless, have already become obvious. Most of you ate breakfast at 7:00 A.M. this morning, when in fact you were eating it at 5:00 A.M."

I continued by saying, "Now this is very important. Do NOT change your clocks to early Tangier time. Please put your clocks back only one hour. Correct information will be stated in the new program. When you are on shore, please do not refer to local time. The time on your wristwatch will be right. Clocks on the ship are, at this moment, being put back electronically one hour." (Luckily or not, the navigator had, in fact, forgotten to do it the previous night.) "The time on your watch and around the ship is now precisely 7:00 A.M.

In your cabins, and posted around the ship, will be a new daily program. This will be available in approximately thirty minutes."

I then apologized most sincerely for the unforgivable error and for any disruption it might have caused. I decided to lighten my remarks with the following:

"Ladies and Gentlemen, because you now have quite a while before going ashore, the following activities will take place: In the cinema, we shall be showing the film *As Time Goes By*. In the Neptune Bar, the navigator has kindly consented to discuss how one navigates a world cruise without the aid of a clock. And in the main lounge, our port lecturer will be repeating his slide show on Tangier. This showing is for those passengers who, when we can get finally get them off, will be too tired to go and see it for themselves."

Some people were understandably upset, but by the end of the day, all was forgiven. This was probably because of the complimentary Casbah cocktail concocted by the bar manager and served all day. The pastry chef had made a large cake for tea in the shape of a clock, and that even at dinner, we served minute steak with complimentary champagne. After leaving Tangier, we had to change the clocks another four times before arriving in New York. The passengers continued to remind me that "time waits for no Mann," especially when he's a cruise director.

Waves of Violence

It is unlikely that you would associate a cruise with a Vincent Price murder mystery, but on one occasion, a cruise along the gentle waves of Alaska's Inland Passage turned to waves of violence.

I will admit that most incidents have happened "below

stairs," in crew areas. A ship is a living city, and within its restrictive area are many nationalities, cultures and religions. Violent incidents are rare, and most ships enjoy a harmonious atmosphere.

This incident was the most violent I have ever experienced at sea. Not only did it happen outside crew quarters, it happened in the most expensive cabin accommodation on a cruise ship, a penthouse suite.

It was at the captain's first private party that I first met Mrs. Mary Clarke. She was an elegant little lady in her late seventies. She had sailed with us before but with her husband, who, unfortunately, had recently passed away. She was accompanied on this eleven-day Alaska cruise by a Mr. Edward Jones. He was in his late fifties and had been a constant traveling companion of the Clarkes for many years.

This was our last cruise to Alaska before we made our way across the Pacific to the Orient. My time was mainly spent in the office, preparing for the long Pacific crossing. I do not remember seeing either Mrs. Clarke or Mr. Jones after that initial evening. We were coming to the end of the cruise, and only the Canadian city of Victoria was left on our itinerary before arriving in San Francisco in two days' time.

The passengers always enjoy Victoria, British Columbia's capital city. It is a city of flowers and fine architecture. The Buchart Gardens is a mecca for all gardeners, as is the Empress Hotel, one of the most impressive hotels in Canada. Unfortunately, we were there for a mere six hours. The ship sailed at 4:00 P.M., making its way into the Strait of Juan de Fuca before sailing south to San Francisco.

The captain's farewell cocktail party was held that evening at 6:45 for all passengers. The guests were always slow in arriving because of the beautiful scenery. Cruising down the strait, with the Olympic Mountain range in Oregon on our port beam, and Vancouver Island on our starboard, makes for a sight few want to miss.

It was a little after 7:00 P.M. when the hotel manager was called away from the party. A few minutes later, he returned, looking very serious, and asked me to get the captain straight away. I took the captain's place in the receiving line as he went to speak with the hotel manager. By the look on the captain's face, I could see something was seriously wrong. This particular captain seemed to have all the problems. His relief enjoyed smooth sailing, but with him—bomb scares, suicides, sea rescues—you name it, he had them! Now what? Without saying anything, he signaled me to announce his farewell speech immediately. At the end of it, he left with the staff captain, and I wound up the proceedings.

It was then that the hotel manager took me aside and said, "There's been a murder in one of the penthouses."

I asked the victim's name and the circumstances. I was shocked when he said it was Mrs. Clarke. Apparently, the butler had found the body. When I told Barbara about the murder, she suggested it might be a good idea if we dropped the word *butler*. The press was bound to make use of the old cliche, "The butler did it."

The captain sent out a letter within the hour to all crew. It stated that no mention was to be made of the deceased's "accident." Anyone divulging the murder would be dismissed from the company. The crew went out of their way to respect Mrs. Clarke's memory and maintain total secrecy.

Later, the hotel manager told me of the events that had transpired that evening. Apparently, the butler was delivering the usual order of caviar and canapes at 6:45 P.M. Jones opened the door and said to him, "She's dead!"

The butler entered the suite and saw, to his horror, the unbelievable sight. The walls, ceiling, and carpet were covered with blood. As he put down the tray, he saw Mrs.

Clarke's body in a black negligee, lying half on the bed, half off. Her head and face were smashed in, and the bed was saturated with her blood. Jones was sitting in a daze, professing to the butler that he had no idea how it had happened. The butler immediately phoned the doctor and then the bridge.

The doctor arrived and pronounced Mrs. Clarke dead. The photographer arrived and took photos. The captain arrived, and Jones was taken to a cabin, where a guard was posted. The penthouse was sealed, and Mrs. Clarke's body was taken to the ship's mortuary. Most cruise ships are equipped with a freezer compartment, as found in mortuaries, in case of a death on board.

The next day, I was in my cabin when my mother-in-law, who was sailing with us at the time, phoned me. Her cabin was two doors up from where they had placed Jones, and she had asked Barbara the evening before, "Why the guard on the cabin door?"

Barbara had told her that a passenger had gotten drunk and had fought with his cabin companion. The captain had decided to keep him locked up until we got to San Francisco.

"Derek," my mother-in-law exclaimed, "that cabin door is open, and both the guard and the man have gone!"

I phoned the staff captain, who is in charge of such matters.

"Jesus Christ!" was his exclamation.

I told my assistant of the situation, and we decided to split up. I took the sun deck, and he started on the Mediterranean deck. There was a general hubbub of activity. Officers were passing us by, communicating with each other on their walkie-talkies. I was walking past a small cocktail lounge, when I saw two of my table companions eating their buffet lunch. Lo and behold, who should be sitting with them but Mr. Jones, the suspected murderer! I decided to keep out of it and phoned the staff captain. I told him, "We've found the leak in the system." Jones was returned to his cabin, and the guard replaced. Apparently, my table companions had made friends with both Mrs. Clarke and Jones. On calling the penthouse, they'd gotten no reply. After making inquiries at the desk, they were told that Mrs. Clarke had had an accident, and Mr. Jones was with her in the hospital. Later, when they happened to be walking along the Mediterranean deck, they saw a sailor sitting outside a cabin door. They asked the Norwegian lad why he was there.

"I have to look after a man who is not well," he said.

They wondered if it was someone they knew. This was their seventeenth cruise with the company, and it was quite possible that they did, especially as, on this cruise, 60 percent of the passengers were repeaters. They were just going to ask the sailor if he knew the name of the passenger, when the door opened. There stood Mr. Jones asking for a cup of coffee. Somehow or other, they talked the guard into letting them take him off for lunch.

The captain had informed the head office and the coroner of the incident. The police boarded in San Francisco, wearing plainclothes so that passengers would not be aware of a problem.

After the ship was cleared, and most of the passengers had left, I was walking through the reception area. Sitting all by himself was Mr. Jones. I was shocked. He looked tired and disheveled. I sat down beside him and asked, "Are you waiting for something, Mr. Jones?"

"Yes, Derek," he replied. "I'm waiting to be arrested."

I could not help but see the irony here. We had a suspected murderer calmly sitting by himself in the main reception area. A few moments later, two plainclothes officers came out of the Purser's Office and took Jones to the police station, where he was formally charged with the murder.

That evening, we set sail for Japan. The penthouse was not to be touched till we left American waters. This was in case the police wished to recheck. It was only then we would be allowed to refurbish the whole apartment.

Two weeks later, the staff captain informed the cruise consultant responsible for sales of future cruises on board that the refurbishing was completed, and the penthouse was ready for occupancy. I was in the penthouse area as the consultant was taking passengers to view the accommodation. A few minutes later, she came out again and took them next door. Both these suites are more or less the same. I came back through the corridor to see the consultant, who was saying good-bye to her clients.

"Did they like it?" I inquired.

Her face looked shocked as she said, "Come and look at this."

I followed her into the penthouse. It looked very good to me. Then she took me to the balcony. Blood covered the area. They had clean forgotten to do just that. The chalked circles and marks the police had used were all over the deck. Apparently, the attack on Mrs. Clarke had started there. Fortunately, the cruise consultant had gone ahead of her clients and, seeing the mess, had made the excuse it had just been painted and was still wet.

We arrived in Hong Kong to receive our first news clippings about the murder. It certainly had made the headlines. Jones claimed he had no knowledge of the murder. He said they had been drinking vodka and champagne that afternoon in Victoria. On returning to the ship, they had bathed and then had taken a nap. When he awoke, he'd found her on the bed—lifeless.

He confessed that he had been an alcoholic all his life but had given up drinking a few months before the cruise. However, he'd started again once they'd set sail. For twenty years, he had not only been Mr. Clarke's social secretary and troubleshooter, he had also been his lover. The Clarkes were millionaires and lived a very social life of which Jones was a part. After Mr. Clarke's death, Jones was a constant companion for Mrs. Clarke and acted as her secretary. Although he shared the penthouse with Mrs. Clarke, he said, "It was a mother-son relationship."

The police questioned Jones for four hours. The evidence showed that Mrs. Clarke had been bludgeoned to death with a champagne bottle. Jones's robe had "significant amounts" of blood on it and looked as if it had been taken off in haste as parts of it were turned inside out. The plot thickened when the police found out that on the first day of the cruise Jones had written out some 420,000 dollars in checks on Mrs. Clarke's account! He'd written a 300,000-dollar check to himself, a 100,000-dollar check that was deposited in a joint account with his roommate, and a 20,000-dollar check to his roommate's son.

After a lot of wrangling as to whether the murder had been committed in Canadian or American waters, it was eventually decided that the trial was America's responsibility. Jones was found guilty of murder and given a life sentence by a San Francisco court. Mrs. Clarke's life was over, and on the thirtieth of August, her ashes were scattered under the Golden Gate Bridge. Only three weeks before, that bridge had been a joyous gateway to her Alaskan adventure; now it was a shroud for her ashes.

A few years later, Mr. Jones died in prison.

The Big Tip

A ship is run like a hotel, and it is therefore a service operation. Of course, paying service operatives high salaries does not automatically garner good service. Rather, good service comes with the hope that passengers will be appreciative in a monetary fashion. You cannot put "Thank you very much" into the bank.

The cruise staff, entertainers, and musicians do not come under the tipping program. However, the biggest tip I have ever seen was given to a musician.

It was late evening on the last day of a cruise that had sailed from San Francisco through the Panama Canal and was now approaching its final destination, Fort Lauderdale. I was sitting in my office when John, my cocktail pianist, came in. Handing a letter to me, he said, "I'd like you to read this." The letter was from a gentleman who was very complimentary about John's piano playing. He said John's talent had been the highlight of his cruise. The last paragraph asked him to accept the enclosed check as a token of his gratitude. I looked up at John and asked "How much is the check?"

He reached into his top pocket and handed it to me. At this point, I must tell you that John was the best jazz pianist I have ever employed on a ship, other than Oscar Peterson and Dave Brubeck, but they were not cocktail pianists. However, no pianist in the history of pianists has ever received such a tip for ticking the ivories, no matter how good they are. The check was for five thousand dollars!

After a moment of surprised shock, I gave the check back to him.

"Can I accept this?" he asked.

"You certainly can," I replied. "I just hope, for your sake, it's met. Do you know who he is?" I asked.

"A guy who is sailing with him says he is a Canadian lumber millionaire and is building a huge home in Florida." John continued to say the man had sat at his piano bar every day. Apparently he loved jazz piano and at one time had himself played in bars. I told John to write him a letter of thanks and to put it under his door that evening.

Two weeks later, John's bank informed him the check had been cleared. He was now five thousand dollars richer. Soon after that, John went on vacation, returning some ten weeks later. He walked into my office in his usual breezy fashion and, after the usual pleasantries, said, "You'll never believe what happened to me a couple of weeks ago."

"Not another check from your benefactor?" I asked.

"Better than that," he said, smiling from ear to ear. "I had only been home a week when I received a letter from my Canadian friend. He said his new home was close to completion, and that he would like me to come over to Florida as his guest for a week and play for the opening parties. The fee was two thousand dollars."

"Well, how did it all go?" I asked.

"Derek, you haven't heard the half of it yet. He gave me the dates and a number to ring in Madrid if I should come. I decided this was an invitation I could not refuse and rang the number. It was his Spanish agent, who told me that when I arrived at the airport I was to go to a special charter desk.

"Two weeks later, I packed my bags and went to the airport. After dealing with all the red tape, I was taken to a section of the airport away from the usual airlines. There were many private jets lined up, the largest of which was the one I boarded. On reaching the top of the steps, I entered a world I have never seen before. I was stunned into silence by the beauty of the interior. The aircraft was just a like a private home. From the vestibule where I stood, I looked into a spacious lounge, in the center of which stood something that took my breath away. It was a baby Steinway grand piano.

"I could not believe my eyes. I walked over to it and saw on the music a note. It read, 'I could not welcome you aboard, John. I thought you might like to practice a little before you

arrived in Florida.' " Now, if anybody's had a better tip, I'd
like to know about it.

Cash and Culture

It would be unusual not to find bingo somewhere in the daily
program. Some cruise ships have a game as often as four
times a day. You can meet some interesting people at a bingo
game during a cruise, especially one on board the *Royal
Viking Star* in 1980.

Shortly before the end of the previous cruise, we had
received, as usual, all the paperwork for this cruise, including
the customary list of VIPs and those to whom the head office
wished us to pay particular attention. The comments beside
the name of Joseph Hirshhorn, an inveterate bingo player,
began by referring to his celebrated position as one of the
leading modern art collectors in the world and as one of the
richest men in America. This is very impressive. We seemed
to be doing well in this area. A few weeks before we had
entertained Walter Annenberg and his family; he had recently given one billion dollars' worth of art to an American
museum. And now, we were to have the pleasure of meeting
Mr. Hirshhorn.

Naturally, we met first at the bingo table. Mr. Hirshhorn
was short in stature, smartly dressed, and in his late seventies. He bought a bingo card from my wife, Barbara. She had
no idea who he was. I mentioned to her, "If money comes to
money, he will win the jackpot." And he did, all $450 of it.
When he came to the table, after we had checked the card,
Mr. Hirshhorn started to count the money.

"I can assure you it is all there, Mr. Hirshhorn," I said.

He continued to count and took no notice of my comment. When he had finished, he slowly looked up and, with

a smile, said, "Mr. Mann, you will never know how much money I have to earn to see this much cash. Let me savor it. Thank you very much."

The next day Mr. Hirshhorn was not playing bingo, but there was a note on the table asking me to call him, which I did. He invited us for a pre-lunchtime drink the next day in his suite.

We arrived to find we were the only couple. Mrs. Olga Hirshhorn and Barbara hit it off, and I was having a fascinating time with Joe, as he had wished me to call him. He told me that he had seen the Wall Street crash coming and had managed to get all his money out a week before. He had made his fortune mainly out of his Canadian uranium mines. We spoke of his amazing art collection which houses the multimillion-dollar collection he gave the nation. Originally, he had wanted the museum built in London or Paris. However, neither city had land available in an area that suited him.

Barbara had asked Olga how she had first met Joe. Apparently, she had been a telephone operator and used to speak to Joe on the phone. He had fallen in love with her voice and had invited her to his beautiful home in Naples, Florida. When she arrived, she was taken by the butler into the garden where Joe was being sculpted by Jacob Epstein. Quite a way to impress a lady!

He asked if we collected art. I said we had several pieces of Russian lacquer paintings. He was not conversant with this delicate art form. So Barbara went and got some pieces from our cabin. He was very much impressed, especially with a brooch on which the face of a Russian princess was painted. He asked Barbara if she would like to sell it. She politely refused his offer, and we continued to enjoy each other's company, so much so that we missed lunch!

The more we talked, the more I was sure I had seen him

before and told Barbara. She lifted her eyes to heaven and replied, "Do we have to go through all that again?" The fact is, I always become distant when this situation arises. I never give up until the mystery is solved. I seldom mention it to the person in question that I feel I have met him or her before. That approach can be embarrassing and makes for uninteresting conversation.

A similar situation had arisen a few months earlier on a South Seas cruise. I was sure I knew the lady at the table next to mine. It took me six days to remember where I had seen her. She was the manager of a dry-cleaning shop next to a bank where I'd worked in North London some twenty-three years before! She was very flattered to be remembered and happy to know her looks had changed very little.

But I digress. Without saying I felt we had met before, I asked Joe, "When you go to London, where do you stay?"

"Usually at the Claridges," he replied.

"Never at the Savoy?" I inquired (I had entertained there).

"No, if we don't stay at the Claridges, we stay with a friend in the country," he said.

"Where would that be, Joe?" I asked.

"I doubt whether you would know the place. It is a ways outside London in Hertfordshire."

"Joe, I lived in Hertfordshire for five years. Know it, I used to drink at the Hoops, one of the best pubs in the area," I said.

"So did I," he exclaimed. "I enjoyed many a glass in that pub with my friend."

"Who is your friend, Joe?" I asked.

"Henry Moore, the sculptor."

That was it! The Hoops and Henry Moore were the answer.

Joe Hirshhorn was Henry Moore's best customer. I knew

101

he had well over two hundred pieces of Henry's work. My favorite is the *Burgers of Calais*. That now stands in the sculpture garden outside the Hirshhorn Museum in Washington.

Joe's art collection has given pleasure to countless thousands, and he brought fame and fortune to many an artist because of his patronage. We were privileged to have known him.

Shortly after Joe passed away, Olga came to visit us on Cape Cod. With an eye for design as acute as her husband's, she advised us on having blinds for our windows rather than curtains. This seemingly minor adjustment transformed the room, and it is still a reminder of the Hirshhorn family, whose company we often enjoyed, and of the game of bingo that rich men sometimes play.

Vincent Priceless

I have always been surprised that such a fine, good-looking man as Vincent Price should have fame with parts involved with terror.

In 1978, Vincent Price and his equally talented wife, Coral Browne, first sailed the Royal Viking Line. In 1989, we had the pleasure of sailing with them again on the new *Royal Viking Sun,* where Barbara and I were hosting the Mariners Club.

Vincent is a genuine authority on art. His is considered one of the finest private collections in America, and his lectures on the subject have been highlights of many a cruise. Vincent shares his name with an artist whose paintings are now commanding a very high price on the investment market, namely, Vincent van Gogh, and his knowledge of this artist revealed in the lectures he gives is particularly riveting.

I first met Vincent and Coral on our northern capitals

cruise. We were visiting Amsterdam, Stockholm, Leningrad, and Oslo. These capitals contain a wealth of art, and who better to guide us through the maze of great painters than Vincent Price?

After Coral and he had settled down in their suite, I asked him if he would like to see me regarding the schedule of talks he was going to give.

He came down to my office, and, with that magnificent voice, said, "Now, Derek, tell me all about yourself and how you came to get this fascinating job."

I told him, and, afterwards, he asked me if I really liked it.

"Vincent," I said, "it is one of the three best jobs in the world.

"What are the other two?" he asked.

"Cruise director on the *Sea* and the *Sky*," I replied.

I noticed all through that cruise his interest in everybody he spoke to. He had a way of making everyone feel special. Rarely speaking of himself, he would readily answer any questions you might have, always bringing the subject back to you.

Before he left my office, I asked him if there was anything I could do to make the cruise more enjoyable.

"Do you happen to know the curator of the Edvard Munch Museum in Oslo?" he asked.

"No, I don't, but I know somebody who probably does," I replied.

Bjorn Kvisgaard was one of the executives of the Norwegian Export Council and had once been on board with us as an enrichment lecturer. He seemed to know everybody in Norway, from the king down.

"What is your interest in Munch?" I asked.

"I would like to see the collection. I own Munch, and many have not been seen by the public."

I told Vincent I would contact my friend and see what he could do. The next day we were in Hamburg, and I managed to get Bjorn on the phone. He knew the curator well (not a big surprise) and said he would arrange everything and pick Vincent up upon our arrival. Alf Boe was the name of the curator, and undoubtedly he would be happy to give Vincent "freedom of the museum."

We sailed down that beautiful entrance to Oslo Harbor, passing many elegant homes and enjoying the striking vista of the city from our Norwegian ship. I remember our managing director escorting us in his sleek sailing yacht. As soon as the gangway was down, the families of the Norwegian crew came on board. We had not been in Oslo for nearly a year, and there were a lot of happy faces. Bjorn was there with Alf, and soon Vincent was whisked away, as contented as a young boy who had found a new penny.

Edvard Munch is Norway's most famous painter. As a young artist, he had been very reluctant to part with his works but had often been forced to sell them in order to live. The works linked most closely with his emotional life, he kept as long as he could, and many of these paintings vividly show his mental distress. When he died in 1944, he left the works still in his possession to the city of Oslo. Vincent was about to feast on the harvest of riches hanging on the museum walls and lying in its vaults.

I would have liked to have taken advantage of Alf's kind invitation to join them, but it was going to be a busy time for me so I said that I might be able to come the next day. We were staying overnight, much to the pleasure of crew and passengers alike.

We returned to the ship in the early hours of the morning to find Vincent had left a message for Coral. She had the gangway officer pass on the message. Apparently, Vincent was staying the night in Toyen, where the museum was located.

It was lunchtime the next day when Coral phoned me and said Vincent had not yet returned. I said I would phone the museum and find out if he had left.

We were sailing at 3:00 P.M., at which time Vincent slowly walked up the gangway.

"Where on earth have you been?" I asked him.

His tired eyes looked up at me, and he said, "I have spent one of the best nights of my life in this city."

Smiling, I said, "You'd better not let Coral hear you say that."

"I have been with Edvard Munch," said Vincent.

"What! All night?" I exclaimed.

"Since I left you yesterday, until an hour ago, I have seen nearly everything he ever painted."

He passed me by with a sigh, got into the elevator, and went aloft to his suite. There, he probably went straight to bed. If dreams are relative to what you have been seeing, he must have had the most terrible nightmares. Munch can be profoundly disturbing. One need only envision his most striking work, *The Scream*, a ghoulish image of terrified desperation. It is fascinating to think of Vincent, the modern master of mystery and terror, secluded in the Norwegian master's house of anguish.

The next morning Vincent appeared in my office bearing a gift. He had found time to buy me a book on the life and paintings of Edvard Munch.

Vincent was a true Renaissance man of multiple talents and varied artistic interests. We knew, if we ever lost him again, he would be in some museum having a love affair with some artist's paintings. Standing beside him would be a patient curator, and Vincent's equally patient wife would be waiting for him back on the ship.

It was with great sadness that my wife and I heard of Vincent's death. He was a man of great charm and wit. Vincent stood as tall in the world of art as he did in the entertainment industry. He will be sadly missed by both.

HRH

The first time world attention was drawn to the kingdom of Tonga was at the coronation of Queen Elizabeth the Second. That day was not blessed with sunshine but with torrential rain. The drive, all in horse-drawn landaus and coaches from Buckingham Palace to Westminster Abbey, lost much of its color. The drenched crowds, who had waited patiently all along the route for some days, cheered the leaders of many nations and royal families from the greatest to the smallest monarchies. All the carriages were covered, save for one, Queen Salote's of Tonga. Her Majesty's courage was only equalled by her size; she weighed some four hundred pounds. Sitting beside her was her aide-de-camp, a minute figure.

As the carriage passed a private residence in a terrace adjacent to the mall, a collection of interested people were gathered to watch this historic occasion. One of the party, a gentleman of no mean size himself, asked, in a condescending manner, who the "girl" was in the landau. He was answered by none other than Noel Coward.

"That *girl* is Queen Salote of Tonga."

"Then who's the man sitting beside her?"

"That's her lunch," replied Noel.

So much for *noblesse oblige*.

Now, that is by no means the end of the story. I just happened to mention it for three reasons: first, it is the true rendition of a story that is told many times when the name

106

Tonga comes up; second, certain social attitudes have not changed; and third, this exchange segues nicely into my story about the queen's grandson.

His Highness Prince Tupoutoa of Tonga is heir to the throne. His father, the king, was a guest at the wedding of Prince Charles and Lady Diana. His Majesty was an impressive figure at that historic occasion.

We were spending a season cruising in the South Seas. The crown prince was on one of the cruises as an enrichment lecturer and honored guest of the Royal Viking Line. He was going to talk about his country, its history, and its people. The prince is an elegant and cultured person. Educated in England at Eton and Sandhurst, he speaks with an aristocratic British accent. He does not rest on his royal laurels but serves as Tonga's minister of defense and foreign secretary. He has a vast background to complement both offices.

I liked him right from the start. He has a good sense of humor, and it was displayed when he informed me of his dislike of public speaking. He said that if I would cancel his program, he would use his influence to get me a knighthood, I had to refuse and remind him that his invitation on board had been extended to him for his oratorial skills. He did very well, and the passengers liked him. Warm and friendly, especially to Americans, who are not used to royalty, he added luster to the cruise. HRH (as he would let us call him in private) loved jazz. In fact, he was an accomplished jazz pianist himself. He enjoyed the American jazz quartet we had in the nightclub.

The cruise was coming to an end. HRH was ending his tour in Tonga. The night before we arrived, he came into my office and invited all my staff and the jazz quartet to his private island for lunch and drinks. Naturally, we were all delighted at this invitation. I told the band after their session that night, and they were thrilled.

We docked in Tonga on a very hot morning and waited for the ship to be cleared. The famous Tonga Police Band was welcoming us with a selection from "Easter Parade," not a bad choice, for it was Easter Sunday. HRH told me that a launch would be coming to pick us up at ten-thirty and that we should be sure to bring our bathing costumes. The time arrived, and I was making way to the dock when I saw, to my amazement, that the quartet were wearing tuxedos in the blazing sun. All the others were dressed in attire suitable for a desert island party.

I explained to the guys that this was not a performance and that they should dress casually. Well, they went back to the ship and came back dressed a little more like it. However, Stanley, the pianist and leader, still wore a suit. What more could I say?

We boarded the launch and made our way to an island fit for a king; ta, bending palm trees, a beach of golden sand, and a crystal-blue sea full of tropical fish. We were about three miles from the main island; the *Royal Viking Star* and the *Royal Palace* were dominant on the skyline.

HRH was on the jetty waiting to greet us. He was relaxed, wearing shorts and a Tongan shirt, but even in those clothes we felt his presence as a royal personage. He took us around a circle of huts covered in palm leaves to an area where they were cooking a pig in a palm-leaf-covered trench. HRH told us that this was going to be the best pork we had ever tasted, and that we were in the presence of the best chef in the South Seas, as was later proved. We went back to a covered area, where HRH had set up a bar with a long table. We'd agreed in advance that we would take turns talking to our host while we enjoyed our food and drinks, so that everybody would get a chance to sit beside him and enjoy his company.

After a magnificent lunch, we started to leave the table

for a swim. Suddenly, we were turned into stone when we heard the aloof voice of formally suited Stanley, as he pointed to the small huts in the circle, ask HRH, "Which one of those huts do you live in?"

His Royal Highness, not flinching an eyelid, replied, "I don't live in one of those. I live over there." Stanley looked in the direction HRH was pointing and saw a palatial estate on the main island. He turned his heads towards the prince and, with a face completely expressionless, said, "Oh, shit."

As the sun started to set, we made our way to the jetty with HRH. He graciously thanked us for being his guests on a day none of us will forget, least of all, Stanley, who learned that royalty is gracious, warm, and magnanimous, especially when you are wearing a suit at a beach party.

Cultural Spread

One of the most interesting cruises and certainly one of the most exciting ever created by Royal Viking Line was its Pacific memories. For many years, Barbara had arranged a World War II veterans' meeting on every cruise, and she still does. From this little acorn, a great cruise grew. We were very fortunate to have the service of Robert Reynolds, head of Valor Tours. He set up a great deal of the hundred and one details to create such an experience, and the expertise of our marketing and associated departments did the rest.

In 1985, the *Royal Viking Star* sailed from Sydney, Australia, with 660 passengers, most of whom were veterans of the Pacific war. Our guests of honor included the former chairman of the Joint Chiefs of Staff, Adm. Thomas C. Moorer; Gen. William C. Westmoreland, former chief of staff for the army; and Vice Admiral Edwin Wilson. A host of other high-ranking officers were also found in a distinguished passenger list.

Many meetings were held for the various units and specialist services on the cruise. The stories were at times not only spine tingling but humorous. A meeting was held for all those who had been at Pearl Harbor on December 7, 1941. There were about thirty passengers present, and the first question asked was, "What was your immediate reaction when the attack started?"

Mrs. Thomas Moorer, the admiral's wife, brought humor to the event. She told the group she had grabbed the three most important things—her children, a bunch of bananas, and a roll of toilet paper—then fled out of the house into the cornfield.

At another meeting, Mr. Larry Adler, the harmonica virtuoso, told quite a different story. He had spent a great deal of his war service entertaining the American forces in the Pacific. After following the marines in at Iwo Jima (where he entertained them in their foxholes), he moved on to Saipan. There, he was asked to do something that we would never forget.

The Japanese had informed the islanders that if they were captured by the Americans, they would be tortured, then killed. The officer in charge asked Larry and two companions if they would read a message to the hundreds of inhabitants who had been congregating on top of an eight-hundred-foot cliff. The message was written phonetically in Japanese for them to read clearly.

Larry, with the aid of a bullhorn, read the message to the islanders. The message pleaded with them not to jump and commit suicide. However, it was to no avail. To their horror they looked on helplessly as some three thousand men, women, and children jumped to their deaths onto the rocks and into the sea below.

On this trip, we were to experience many new islands not previously visited by the Royal Viking Line. All of them were areas where the war had played a prominent part. Manus is one of these islands. It lies in the Admiralty chain of Papua, New Guinea. During the war, the island provided the site for a huge naval and air base, built by the Americans. After the war, everything had been abandoned. Today, many rusting remnants of American equipment are still visible.

As we sailed into the harbor, we noticed hundreds of the native population crowding the jetty and landing area. We were the first cruise ship of our size to have sailed there, and probably our visit was the most exciting thing that had happened to them since the end of the war. It was not possible to dock, so we anchored out. The tenders were lowered, and the first one was captained by Bjorn Olsen, a Norwegian officer, known for his ready wit, sense of humor, and fluent English. The top brass—Vice Admiral Wilson, who had been stationed at Manus, Admiral Moorer, and General West-moreland—were on Olsen's tender.

Admiral Wilson was pointing out interesting areas that had once housed thousands of men and equipment. As he did so, we saw quite a few small boats coming out to meet us. They were filled with the locals, fleshing out the scene in their finest dress. One of their boats was larger than the rest. It was covered with rust and filled to the gunnels with scrap iron. It looked like a floating junkyard.

Bjorn addressed his prominent passengers, saying, "Gentlemen, I think you are going to like this."

With that, he pulled the wheel over in the direction of the oncoming boat, throttled back the engines, and slowly started to come alongside. The natives looked at us inquisitively with not a smile on their faces, as Bjorn leaned across the admiral and called out, "Do you have any Grey Poupon?"

When Everyone Is Somebodee

One particular cruise in the South Seas was enhanced by more than 150 members of the very prestigious European Club. Many of the members were titled, from princes to counts, from lords and barons, to knights and dames. To top it off, we had several high-ranking Americans on board, namely, a former chief of staff, three admirals, two generals, and an ambassador. It was a very impressive passenger list.

We were into the second week. It was Sunday morning, and I had just finished the church service and was making my way up the stairs to give a port talk in the main lounge. I reached the top of the stairs as two elderly ladies were making their way down.

"Aren't you going to listen to the port talk?" I asked.

"No, we don't want to listen to the pope talk, dear; we're not Catholic."

It must have appeared to them that everyone who was anybody was on board, so why not the pope!

The rest of the day found me cheerfully singing Gilbert and Sullivan:

> "To this conclusion we agree,
> When everyone is somebodee,
> Then no one's anybody!"

Russian Interludes

Cruising in the North Sea and the Baltic offers the traveler a wealth of different nations, representing vastly different cultures and varied scenery. Most of these places favor the democratic way of life, and entry to them by cruise ship is fairly smooth. However, Leningrad (formerly and presently

Saint Petersburg), the most interesting place in many ways, could be more difficult, depending on the political climate.

I first sailed into that harbor in 1975 on the *Royal Viking Sea*. The ship had been completed in 1973 and was a floating palace. Gleaming white and beautiful, she tied up at a grubby, shabby dock. We were greeted by a few officials and ten border guards. Intourist, headed by a gentleman named Mischa, was the organization responsible for the excursions.

We greeted them with customs and immigrations forms in the card room and started the usual process. The chief purser had confirmed all prearranged requirements, so clearance went smoothly. Mischa informed me that he had asked a professor of cconomics from Leningrad University to speak to the passengers the next day at 4:00 P.M. That was fine by us, and I scheduled it in the daily program for the next day. For our first call, everything was working very well, and all of us were quite impressed with the whole setup.

The next day, they invited the ship's executives to a luncheon at an old restaurant in the Nevsky Prospect. Eight courses, half a bottle of vodka, and two bottles of wine later, we were poured back onto the ship.

Feeling benevolent, I invited the intourist group to my cabin and opened a bottle of Dom Perignon. They had never heard of it, so I explained a little of its history. They then asked how much a bottle cost. I told them eighty-five dollars. Their faces showed shock, and they put down their glasses and excused themselves politely. The cost of a bottle would support a family in Russia for two months, and that was a bit too much for them to swallow.

I had a few moments left to go down to the main lounge and introduce the professor. He was poorly dressed in a threadbare suit, no tie, his shirt collar frayed at the edges. I really felt embarrassed for the poor man. He spoke well, and his English was a credit to him. However, question time was a joke. Like a good politician, he avoided answering anything that the passengers asked regarding freedom, the Jewish situation, political dissidents, etc.

At the end of it all, I said to Mischa that I would prefer these talks to be interviews. He did not go for that one at all. I mentioned having local entertainment on board. That was also met with a *"Nyet."*

That summer, we had three more calls in Leningrad. I told the captain and the hotel manager that I was going to try my best to get entertainment on board the ship. The Russians always had an evening performance, either at the circus or the ballet, but many of the passengers were elderly and, after a day of sightseeing, were too tired to go out at night.

On our next arrival in Leningrad, we could tell that we had done well on the previous visit. Passengers had spent money like water, and Royal Viking passengers had more to spend than most. Mischa was particularly friendly and invited us all out again, this time to the Astoria Hotel.

For this visit, they had arranged for the passengers to see *Sleeping Beauty,* performed by the Kirov Ballet. However, they could only offer us one hundred seats at one dollar each. We had 545 passengers on board. This was my chance. I asked him what the other 445 passengers were going to do that evening. Could the professor, booked for 4:00 P.M., speak at 9:30 P.M. instead?

"No, he can not," was Mischa's reply.

This was the time for the attack. I then offered Mischa five hundred dollars if he could produce something for the passengers that evening. He smiled and said he would contact his superiors.

I found out later that he had rung Moscow. After lunch, he informed me that members of the performing arts faculty at the Palace of Culture would arrive on the ship at nine that evening.

They were fabulous. It was difficult to believe that they were all amateurs. It was the best variety show I had ever put on a ship. Mischa beamed when they received a standing ovation. I had sandwiches and soft drinks served, then I asked if I might personally show the artists around the ship. At first Mischa was reluctant; but after another large brandy, he relented, and I started my tour.

There were ten of them. Two spoke excellent English and acted as interpreters for the others. Their eyes had never seen such modern luxury. We arrived at the library, and there everything stopped. They became very excited, as one of them started to translate the titles. The reference bookcase got the most attention. Suddenly, they saw Churchill's *History of the Second World War*. It was as if they were looking at the pyramids for the first time.

An English-speaking girl asked me if she could look at it. I took it down from the shelf and gave it to her. Before opening it, she clutched it to her bosom as if she were comforting a child. I knew what I was going to do was wrong, but I just could not stop myself. I took her to one side and told she could have the book. Her face half lit up in a smile. She pulled the book closer to her. I said, "If you want it, the others must not see you take it." Reluctantly, she slowly put the book back, and we left the library to continue the tour.

Later that night, I went on my rounds and came to the library. I walked in and glanced over the books. My eyes fell upon the reference section. They were slightly ajar. I went over and closed them, noticing what I had more or less expected. Winston Churchill had gone to Russia, with a lot of love.

*   *   *

During our calls into Russia, we often opened up the

ship to those much less privileged than ourselves. In so doing, I "helped" to enlighten those who came on board, exposing them to the unimaginable wonders of a luxury liner. However, all this was coming to an end.

We had another trip to make before leaving northern Europe and wending our way south to the Mediterranean. I was saying good-bye to Mischa on the pier, telling him I would see him in two weeks' time. He looked at me with a wry smile and said, "Maybe, but I think it's time you had a holiday."

I thought nothing of the remark until the very next day in Helsinki, when the agent came on board with a telex informing me I must leave the *Sea* and go directly to San Francisco.

I rang my boss from Copenhagen to find out what the reason was. He said the new assistant cruise director on the *Sky* had had cold feet, and I was to take over its Circle Pacific cruise. I asked if this was really the case and whether it had anything to do with the Russian officials. He was quite insistent that no pressure had come from Intourist or anybody else.

It was another three years before I went back to Russia. On arriving in Leningrad, who was on the dock to greet me but Mischa. Kissing me on both cheeks, he smiled and said, "This was quite a long holiday, Derek. I hope you enjoyed it?"

I looked at him and smiled a knowing smile, and he just laughed. I could never prove that he had had anything to do with it, but a situation soon to emerge proved to me it was no coincidence.

We were to make four calls to Leningrad that season, and I decided that this time I was going to see Moscow. Previously, I had never been able to make it, but I was now cruise director and was able to arrange my own schedule.

116

The first thing to do was get a visa. This necessitated going to the Russian Embassy in Copenhagen. The agent arranged for an appointment for me, and after all my duties had been done, I would deal with the visa.

I had said good-bye to all my passengers and was walking back to the front of the passenger terminal from the road. On my right was a public phone box. As I walked by, the phone rang. Being me, I picked it up and said, "This is Copenhagen Steam Laundry." The voice on the other end of the line said, to my complete amazement, "Can I speak to Derek Mann?"

I immediately thought this had be a "Candid Camera" gag and looked around me for some clue as to where the crew might be. There was nobody. The place was deserted. I asked who was speaking. It turned out to be an agent in New York asking me if I would be interested in doing a world cruise for another line. I told them where I was and asked how they had managed to get the number. They said it was the ship's number they had been given by the San Francisco office. I later found out the number on the dock finished with the digits 8, 5. The number on the road phone ended with 5, 8. They had reversed the number when dialing.

Coming back on the ship, telling this unbelievable story to everybody who would listen, I proceeded to get changed for my meeting with the Russians. I arrived at the very sturdy-looking mansion on an elegant street and, walking through a high pair of wrought-iron gates, rang the bell of the front door. It was opened by a Russian gentleman, who looked as if he had just stepped out of a James Bond movie. His square head was shaven, and he was built like a barn door. He did not speak to me. He just looked. I explained who I was. Without taking his eyes off me, he waved me silently into the Embassy. It had neither warmth nor carpets. He showed me into the waiting room, equally uninviting, and then spoke for the first time. "Wait here."

He was gone for about ten minutes, returning through twin doors at the other end of the room, draped with heavy damask curtains. Behind a large imposing desk sat another James Bond Russian. He motioned me to sit down and proceeded to look at the papers I had completed a couple of weeks earlier. "Why do you wish to go to Moscow?" he asked.

"I have never been and would like to see it. Also, I want to act as escort for our group."

He then looked at some other papers I did not recognize. Without lifting his head, he just said, "Denied."

With that, the twin doors opened right on cue, and the other member of the staff beckoned me out into the hallway, through the front door, and out into the free world.

I was now quite certain that my "holiday" had been arranged in 1977, and I was not very comfortable about the situation.

At this time, there was an elderly couple who had, so far, spent some thirteen months on board the ship! I had even put a Georgian doorway in front of their suite with their names and their arrival date on it. They were very wealthy and wanted to spend some time outside the United States for tax reasons. Their son ran the family business, which involved buying banks, buildings, and various worldwide investments. Rupert, as we shall call him, was flying in regularly from all over the world to have meetings with his father. He would arrive by helicopter, private jet, and, in some cases, the company yacht. His influence seemed to have no bounds, and he was on intimate terms with many world leaders.

As I was coming up the gangway, returning from my unsuccessful trip to the embassy, who should be coming down but Rupert. After exchanging a few pleasantries, I told him I was not going to be able to escort his mum and dad to Moscow. I let him know of my short interview and the outcome.

"Give me your passport," he said.

No sooner had I given it to him than he ran down the gangway, saying he would see me later.

You probably have guessed the outcome. On his return, he gave me my passport, in which was stamped a visa for visiting Moscow. He refused to discuss the matter, except to say he had rung a friend, who had somebody ring the Soviet Embassy.

We arrived in Leningrad a few days later, and I was ready to go with my group of fifty passengers. First, we had to go through a special immigration procedure in the small lounge. The inspector's name was Ivan, a character not even Mischa liked. He never smiled and was a pain in the proverbial. After all the passengers had had their documents stamped, it was my turn.

I gave him the passport, and, with hardly a glance at the visa, he said, "Out of date."

They had fooled Rupert and me. I knew the dates were clear in the application because the copy was attached, and I showed him. He pointed to the stamp that showed the visa had run out the day before. The passengers were upset, and Rupert's parents refused to go unless I did. Some other passengers took up the cause, and, with that, the Terrible left the room.

Fortunately, there was another member of the shore excursion staff whose visa was okay, and I managed to talk all but Rupert's parents into going to Moscow. To this day, I have never found out whether Rupert knew he had been duped. I have a feeling it might have been the first time, and I certainly was not going to be the one to tell.

* * *

After thwarted efforts to get to Moscow, I seldom went on shore to look in the dollar stores for the beautiful Russian lacquer boxes. These fine works of art have become collectors' items over the years, and I prize my collection above all else. My feelings toward the Russian authorities were not cordial, although I always showed respect and acted in a manner so as to not "rock the boat."

We had two trips to take before leaving for the "warmth" of the Mediterranean. On board this cruise was a Russian lady whom we shall call Natasha. Her purpose in coming on this cruise back to her native land was to visit her husband's grave. He had died shortly after the war and was then buried outside Leningrad. She had left Russia a few years later and gone to live in the United States.

On our arrival in Leningrad, I put her in touch with Mischa, who had handed her request to Ivan the "bloody" Terrible. Later that evening, I saw Natasha coming into the lounge from the deck. She looked in a bad way and had obviously been drinking. I sat her down and found out that they would not allow her to go to her husband's grave. No reason had been given. She was very overwrought, and I decided to call the doctor. It was while we were waiting that she started to talk about suicide. When the doctor arrived, I told him of her remarks.

Later that evening, as I made my way back to my cabin, I noticed an able seaman seated outside a passenger's door. I asked him what he was doing there, and he told me there was a passenger who was not well and the captain wanted to make she did not leave her room.

Most of the suicides I have experienced at sea are usually of the overboard variety. It is a strange thing, but most of these cases leave the same sign: their shoes are left by the rail.

I always dread seeing shoes left by themselves on the deck and, especially, close by the rail. So I understood why the captain had arranged the surveillance. I realized that the doctor had given the widow a sedative to ensure a good night's sleep.

The next day, the captain and the hotel manager made a personal request to Soviet immigration, hoping it might change their minds. It was fruitless. Immigration was adamant and refused to discuss any reason for the denial. The hotel manager went to see Natasha and told her of the company's efforts.

We sailed from Leningrad at 5:00 P.M. and made our way through that busy port and out into the Baltic. I had just finished the evening show when I saw Natasha making her way over to me. Once again, she had been drinking heavily and was in a bad state. Earlier, the doctor had told me she was calm, and he was letting her go down to dinner.

I got her to sit down beside me and asked one of my staff to contact the nurse. Natasha was sobbing quietly and, through her sobs, reaffirmed her desire to do away with herself that very evening unless she could visit her husband's grave. She did not seem aware that we had sailed. I got one of my staff to call the nurse and, when she arrived, told her of Natasha's suicide threat. The nurse took her back to her cabin, strewn with money, clothes, and other paraphernalia, and called the doctor. He gave her a strong sedative, and once again, a member of the ship's company was posted outside her door.

During the night, the nurse called in to see if all was well. Her last call was at 5:00 A.M. At 7:30 A.M., the stewardess went into the cabin to seen whether Natasha was okay and to ask whether she would like some breakfast. As she appeared to be fast asleep, the stewardess did not wake her. At 8:30 A.M., the nurse arrived and was told by the stewardess that she had just gone in, but the lady was still fast asleep. The nurse decided to take a look and see if the passenger was awake. The first thing she noticed was how tidy the room was, and she remarked as much to the stewardess, who assured the nurse that the room was the same at 7:30 A.M. The nurse was perplexed because, when she had come in at 5:00 A.M., the room had been cluttered.

Walking through the eerily clean cabin, the nurse reached the bed and gently shook the sleeper. There was no response. The passenger was cold. In fact, Natasha was dead.

On the dressing table lay four envelopes. Two of them enclosed tips for the stewardess and the waiters. Another envelope was for the captain, saying how sorry she was for the trouble she had caused, and the last one was for her husband's sister in Oregon, stating the obvious and enclosing money, travellers' checks, and the unused portion of her return air ticket.

Natasha had died of an overdose. She had brought tablets with her, fully prepared to finish her life. I somehow feel that she knew all along this was going to be the outcome, and her departure from this world was as clinical and deliberate as the behavior of the Russians who had compelled it.

Call of the Wild?

Over the years, I have spent most of my summer seasons cruising in Alaska. At the time of this writing, I am looking forward to another in those breathtakingly beautiful waters.

Most of the time, we start our Alaskan adventure from Vancouver, British Columbia. This elegant city has a beautiful harbor from which to sail north to Alaska. Our course takes us through a maze of islands and channels that make up the Inland Passage. This waterway is a beautiful alterna-

With Barbara and Cary Grant on the Royal Viking Sky's 1983 World Cruise.
(Courtesy of Royal Viking Line)

Enjoying Captain Vebenstad's Party with Mr. and Mrs. Vincent Price. *(Courtesy of Royal Viking Line)*

On the right, His Royal Highness Prince Tupoutoa of Tonga. On the left, Peter Longley my friend and then assistant, now cruise director, of the QE2. *(Courtesy of Royal Viking Line)*

Fred Goerner, broadcaster, producer, author, and my best man when Barbara and I married in the chapel on the Royal Viking Star in 1980. *(Courtesy of Royal Viking Line)*

A memorable team of staff and entertainers on The Royal Viking Star's 1978 World Cruise. (*Left to right:*) Sasha Abrams, Susan Povey, Derek Povey, Ray Avon, Peter Alexander, Elaine Avon, myself, Barbara, Tommy and Beryl Plummer, Roy and Joyce Edwards; (center:) Martin Snowdon. *(Courtesy of Royal Viking Line)*

Gary Oakes and Lou Garcia production of "The King and I" on the Royal Viking Sky's 1983 World Cruise. All the costumes were made of Thai silk by Barbara and her team on board, as was the scenery. *(Courtesy of Royal Viking Line)*

(Left to right:) Lou Garcia, Gary Oakes, Barbara, myself, Carmen and Andreas Torres (Los Malagas). No cruise director could ever wish for two finer teams of artists and producers. *(Courtesy of Recency Cruises and Trans Ocean Photos)*

Our last photo taken on the Royal Viking Star in December 1986 with Peter and Captain Ola Harsheim, one of cruising's finest captains. *(Courtesy of Royal Viking Line)*

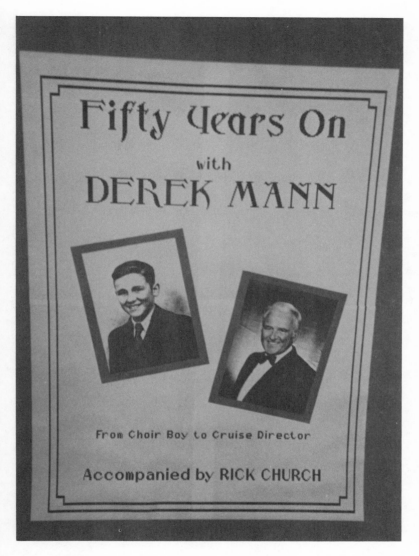

The poster celebrating my fifty years in show business on the Regent Sea's Circle South America cruise, Nov. 28th, 1993. *(Courtesy of Regency Cruises and Trans Ocean Photos)*

With Donald O'Connor at the Costume Ball on the Royal Viking Star. *(Courtesy of Royal Viking Line)*

tive to that of the Pacific Ocean, with which it runs parallel for a thousand miles. At its end, lies Skagway, the gold rush town of '98 and the gateway to the Yukon.

The Inland Passage is lined with literally billions of trees and magnificent mountain scenery. At one part, in Canadian waters, you pass the Indian town of Bella Bella, which involves itself mainly in fishing and forestry. Before coming to this settlement, the passage narrows considerably, and, in the trees, the symbol of America nests, the bald eagle. This stately bird is no stranger to this area, and from time to time we would make a sighting as they sat high in the branches of the pine tree.

As we make our way through these narrows, I give a commentary from the bridge. I point out the sights and speak about the history and culture of the Bella Coola Indian. The Canadian pilot, with others, keeps a lookout for eagles. With so many trees, they are not always easy to point out.

On this particular cruise, we had just entered this stretch of narrow water, when the pilot sighted an eagle high up in a smaller tree. The background was full of higher trees, making the sighting difficult. The decks were full of people, as I made an announcement. "There is an eagle on top of that small tree in line with the white mountain peak," I said excitedly.

I could hear the passengers by the bridge saying, "Where? Where is it? Where did he say it was?"

I knew it was difficult to see, so I asked the captain if he would give a blast on the ship's whistle. On the few occasions we had done that, it had worked like a charm. The eagle would take off in majestic flight, much to the pleasure of the passengers.

"Ladies and gentlemen, in an effort for you to see the eagle, the captain is going to blow the ship's whistle. You'll then be able to see it in flight. For those of you on the starboard side, keep your eyes on the front part of those six large trees by that inlet."

The captain gave a good, loud blast. Not a movement from the bird.

"Well, I don't think he heard that one, so let's try again," I said.

The captain gave three quick blasts. Not a sausage. The eagle started to preen itself, oblivious of our presence.

In a voice full of disappointment I said, "Ladies and gentlemen, it seems we have come across the only deaf bald eagle in the Canadian wild."

* * *

Farther north in Alaskan waters, there is a stretch of water called Icy Strait. It is here that many whales, mostly humpbacks, feed on the krill and plankton that abound in this area. Whales migrate north in the late spring to feed on the wealth of food in these Alaskan waters. They come from Baja, California, and also from the Hawaiian Islands. Not many of us travel thousands of miles to visit our favorite seafood restaurant.

Within Icy Strait is Adolphus Point, where we would arrive in the early evening. The whales would slowly surface around us, their blow holes sending a jet of water into the air, as if in greeting. Just as slowly, they would dive down, their finlike tails flapping the water in self-applause, as they disappeared from sight.

Before we got to Adolphus Point, I would start my commentary from the bridge. I would tell the passengers that the first signs of life would be Fred and Gladys. I had named these two whales years ago. It was an extraordinary coincidence that these two whales had always been traveling four hundred yards from the shoreline every time I had been there. Only once in thirty calls did they not appear. Many times the whales would be all around us, some of them mating. When I sighted this intimate act, I would jokingly ask the passengers to look the other way. "Let's face it," I would say, "you wouldn't want people watching you, now would you?"

Whales have a habit of *breaching*, that is, they project themselves out of the water. No one has yet worked out the reason for this amazing act. To see some fifty tons of whale doing this, throwing off a huge volume of water that would cascade out around them, then crash back, is a sight you don't easily forget.

We were off Adolphus Point one evening with another ship (which shall remain nameless) that was carrying only 150 passengers and was marketed as an adventure, wildlife cruiser. All of a sudden, close to the vessel, a whale started to breach, not once but continually. I looked through my glasses along their rail to see how their passengers were enjoying the show. There was no one in sight. I could not believe it! For a "wildlife adventure" ship sailing right in the middle of one of nature's showcases, it was inconceivable that nobody was there. I decided to call the ship on the marine radio.

"This is the *Regent Sea* calling [the name of the ship]. Come in, please."

"This is . . . ," a voice replied.

"Are you aware that you have a whale continually breaching on your aft port quarter and not one passenger is in sight?" I asked incredulously.

"Yes, thank you," he said. "We have told them, but they are down below having dinner. With the crowd we have this week, you could put on a crucifixion and they'd still prefer to eat."

*   *   *

135

Since adding Sitka to our Alaskan schedule, we now pass that area late at night. However, last year, for two cruises, we passed Adolphus Point during the day, and I am pleased to say that Fred and Gladys did not disappoint the passengers or, more importantly, the cruise director, a passing acquaintance of theirs for many years.

A Cabin Not up to Scratch

If you came home one night and found a person sitting in chair, refusing to leave, how would you react? On a ship, your cabin is your home, the only place you can get away from it all and have some privacy. It is seldom invaded. But on one sailing day out of New York, I had an uninvited guest.

The ship had sailed, making its way up the Hudson River. I had paid my respects to the Statue of Liberty and had decided to go down and rest before the evening's festivities. As I walked toward my cabin, I noticed that the door was slightly ajar. I assumed that my steward was simply turning down the bed. On entering, I discovered instead a very large lady, weighing at least three hundred pounds, sitting on my bed. She wore a multicolored woolen overcoat, long leather boots, and a small hat perched on her head, sporting a flower that resembled a daisy that was bending toward her brow.

"What are you doing in my cabin?" I politely asked.

"What do you mean, 'your' cabin?" she indignantly answered. "This is *my* cabin, man." (I nearly asked her how she knew my name.)

"Madam, I am a staff member on this ship, and this is not a passenger cabin; it's a staff cabin," I stated firmly.

"What does this say?" she said, thrusting a passenger ticket in front of my nose. There, plainly printed on the ticket, was my cabin number. Someone had screwed up the ticketing.

"Obviously, there's been a mistake," I said.

"Well, I'm not moving; I like this cabin," she replied, surveying the premises.

The situation was becoming a stalemate, so I told her I was going to see the chief purser, and I left. The purser apologized for the error and gave me a key to another cabin for the passenger. The new cabin was one deck up and was a nice outside double, which she would get at no extra cost. I returned to my cabin with the good news.

"I don't want an upgrade! I want this cabin," she stated firmly.

"But won't you just come up and look at it? It's really very nice, and you have a porthole." She was not impressed.

"These are all my things in here, the pictures, everything. It's my home," I told her, getting more frustrated.

"Well, you can take them upstairs to the other cabin," she flatly stated.

I realized I was wasting my time, so I returned to the purser. "If she won't get out peacefully, then we'll have to drag her out," was his comment.

He phoned for the he heavy brigade. The heavy brigade was really heavy. Dave was 250 pounds, six foot four, and gay. Passengers never knew, but we had all learned to love and admire his magnificent gowns at the crew bar. His rank was that of able seaman, and so he was when it came to matters requiring some force.

Dave arrived, and we apprised him of my predicament. He smiled and said, "No problem." Dave suggested I go to the Crow's Nest Bar and wait for him there. Only fifteen minutes had passed when Dave, his friend Reg, and the nurse came into the bar.

"There you are," Dave said, giving me my key. "She's out."

"Already," I said incredulously. "How on earth did you manage it?"

"Simple," he said. "I took the nurse and Reg with me."

"Why did you take the nurse?" I asked.

"So she would tell her what the problem was."

"And what was that?" I inquired.

"Your disease," he said, as if I knew.

"What disease?" I asked.

"Scabies," he stated.

"I don't have scabies," I insisted.

"Well, you do now, just for a few days," he said with a smile.

I brought them a drink and got the full story. Dave could not see himself dragging a lady out of the cabin by force, especially that one. He remembered being told by a ship's doctor of a similar situation and of how they had dealt with it.

After leaving me, he got his friend Reg to get the fumigating equipment from the housekeeper while he rang for the nurse. When they were all assembled, he knocked on the door. The voice from within called out, "I ain't leavin' this cabin."

The nurse identified herself and asked the lady to open the door. She did and was confronted with one very large sailor, another one with a lot of spray equipment, and the ship's nurse. Nurse Dates said they had been informed of the situation but before any move was made, she wanted to warn the lady of the problem the previous tenant had, which could possibly affect her health. "Mr. Mann has been complaining of an irritation in his hands and just this morning went to a skin clinic in New York." They had received the results immediately before sailing. "Mr. Mann has scabies, a skin disease that is easily transmitted. If you wish to stay in this cabin, we shall have to fumigate it completely and take out the bedding and carpeting," she said seriously.

The lady, apparently, bounded to her feet, grabbed a large purse and carpetbag, and left with Dave to inspect the other cabin. There she stayed for the rest of the cruise, having been irritated only by the hassle and the constant nervous scratching of her hands.

To Alaska with Love

Don't be led into thinking that there is only one "Love Boat." Every ship that carries passengers can boast that title. In the late seventies, I was cruise director for the Alaska season, sailing out of California. We left Los Angeles on a Saturday and sailed north to Alaska. Thirteen days later, we returned to San Francisco to disembark passengers and pick up new ones. From there, we sailed south to Los Angeles and, after the same procedure, returned to the final frontier.

It was my first season in Alaska, the first of many to what the Aleuts rightly call "the Great Land." It is one of the most impressive areas of the world I have seen and offers the traveler a wealth of scenery, history, and culture. The Inland Passage from Vancouver is a magnificent prelude to the mountain ranges and hundreds of glaciers that abound in that last frontier so many Americans have not yet traveled.

Our company, by virtue of its cost and position in the marketplace, attracted mainly the elderly, wealthy American. We were, therefore, rather surprised to see so many younger people on board, especially of the female gender. It became apparent within a short space of time that they were there for two reasons: one, to see Alaska; and two, to propagate the species—the latter taking preference.

The ship's doctor had a theory about these exciting phenomena. Most of the ladies hailed from California, and he reckoned they were being sexually frustrated by their geographical location. Gay liberation had not made life easy for the "straight" female. The cry seemed to be, "Go north, young lady," and quite a few were doing just that, fortunately, on our ship!

The first cruise went very well in every respect. The comment cards showed figures well above average, and the management was very happy. So were the crew.

On the third night out, I was cunningly seduced by a pretty girl from San Francisco. She was my "first encounter of the California kind." She rather felt I had come with the fare. The fact that she had paid for a cabin in which to hang her clothes did not faze her one bit.

I was sorry to see her leave. However, life at sea does not allow relationships to blossom, unless you are together on board for many months at a time. I alluded to this subject elsewhere.

This first cruise had been very busy in more ways than one, and things would have to slow down, otherwise I was not going to survive the season. Many of the crew had the same feeling.

We boarded new passengers in San Francisco for our second cruise and made our way down to Los Angeles. Once again, there was an abundance of young ladies. Many of them were travel agents on a familiarization cruise. Our job on board was to "familiarize" them with the operation and, hopefully, with us.

A cocktail party was held to welcome them. They mentioned to us that, when taking calls from prospective passengers, they were often asked if our ships were like the "Love Boat," a question they could never quite answer. When they arrived back in San Francisco, most of them would!

I blush when I tell you I had another "problem" on this cruise. Her friend had informed her I was normal, a fact she was anxious to confirm. Fortunately, her passions peaked at lunchtime, when the food of love replaced the buffet. Sex gave her a thirst, and the rest of the afternoon she quenched it at the bar. She was seldom seen at dinner or at the shows and would never tell me where she went. For me, the arrangement was perfect. I was on a forced diet, and the evening was free for my other activities.

The cruise came to an end, and, after the passengers had disembarked, I received a call from a "high-ranking officer." He requested my presence in his cabin as soon as I was free. Apparently, according to him, I had been invading his "territory" (his term not mine) on this last cruise. To avoid unpleasantness, I told him I was not aware of it and apologized—respectfully. He said, "In the future, as these cruises are busier 'socially' than most, I will let you know when I have decided on my choice and to whom I will give the pleasure of my company."

As I was leaving his quarters, I could not help but notice a pair of ladies' panties protruding from under the mattress of his bed. What made them more interesting was the fact that I knew them intimately, but only at lunchtime!

The CD's Dilemma

There is no doubt that the job of cruise director, especially on a ship of high prestige and luxury, is looked upon by many as the ultimate occupation. Most cruise directors are reasonably attractive people, and the occasional romance takes place—again and again.

One night, I returned to my cabin to find a stark naked lady of unbelievably large proportions in my bed. She refused to leave unless I fulfilled my duty as cruise director. She thought that sex, with same, was included in the fare. If the bed had had room for two, things might have been different. However, after making it clear that I was not available, I called the officer of the watch. He found it difficult to understand why I should want him to come down and get her out. I suggested he might like to take her to his own cabin instead. Unfortunately, he had just come on duty. To cut the story short, it was only after calling her daughter, who was traveling with her, that the daughter and I managed to get her mother out of the cabin. After meeting the daughter, I wished she had been the one I had found. I wouldn't have had to call the officer of the watch.

Another time we were cruising the Australian coast, making our way up to Cairns. I arrived back in my cabin after a long day at sea. Taking off my clothes, I went into the shower. I was not alone. Standing behind the shower curtain was a very attractive Australian girl, wearing only a smile. In circumstances like this, there was no need to call the officer of the watch; he was clean enough already. So I did the only thing possible. I turned on the water.

One can laugh at these situations, but sometimes they are far from funny. A cruise director friend of mine was sailing out of Copenhagen to the North Cape. On board was a lady in her early thirties, not very attractive, and proving to be a problem to her travel group. Her attitude and behavior were strange, but she seemed to be harmless.

She started to show some interest in the ship's doctor, but when he produced his wife, she backed off. Her attentions turned to my cruise director friend. She followed him around like an adoring puppy. He acted in a proper manner and was courteous and patient with her attitude. Her fixation became worse. She told him that she was madly in love with him and built up great fantasies about their future life together.

He decided to take her out to lunch in the next port. Away from the ship, he felt it would be easier to explain his situation, to explain that he was seriously spoken for. He told her that her attentions would have to be in another direction. Lunch was a disaster. She would not take no for an answer. She started yelling and eventually ran out of the hotel and into the street.

Back on the ship, she phoned his office, apologizing for her behavior. Early the next morning, he got a call from his assistant saying the office was in a shambles. The photos of his girlfriend had been torn from the wall, papers from the desk were scattered on the floor, and everything was a mess. His crazy friend had broken in. The following day, her continuous bombardment of his work continued. He was giving a talk in the cinema when she suddenly started screaming at him on the stage. He had to cancel the talk. The next day she punched him in the ribs in front of the passengers.

Normally, we try to deal with problems ourselves without bringing in higher management. However, this little drama was getting out of control and becoming public. He decided to report the situation to the hotel manager, who was not very sympathetic, feeling the infatuation would blow over. It didn't. Since my friend thought this was a mental problem, he decided to see the doctor. The doctor, who had also experienced the advances of this woman, decided to tell the captain.

The cruise director left the doctor's office for the broadcasting center to do his radio show. About ten minutes into the broadcast, the woman scorned broke in and started smashing up the tapes and equipment. She left screaming and shouting obscenities.

It was obvious that this person might well become suicidal. My friend contacted the captain and the doctor, telling them of the latest event and warning them that they had better start to take the situation seriously.

The captain asked him to get the woman to come and see him. He also asked to make sure the doctor was present. My friend saw her making her way into the main lounge and asked her nicely to come with him to the captain's quarters. She flatly refused and ran screaming out onto the deck. She was finally caught and put under guard in her cabin. Her group leader was then contacted and went down to her cabin. She was greeted with cries from her tempestuous charge that in her scorned state she was going to burn down the cabin and slash her wrists. The doctor was called and, with the help of three sailors, she was sedated. She was taken down to the hospital. They had one hell of a time with her the following day. She was taken off the ship in the next port and put into the hospital. She escaped from there three hours later.

That evening at sea, my friend had a call from a relative of the woman's, telling him he was the only one who could save the woman's life. He explained, regretfully, that there was nothing he could do under the present circumstances. Two days later he received a telegram from the escaped patient, begging him to ring a number in Copenhagen. The telegram was addressed to Mr. Sunshine, Lollipops, and Rainbows.

He did not phone and, to this day, has never heard another word. It goes to show that the job of a cruise director is not all sunshine, lollipops, and rainbows. There can be raindrops as well.

Restroom Adventure

I have constantly admired in the elderly, and especially those with some form of physical disability, their tenacity when it comes to travel. I have seen a man eighty-nine years old walking on two canes in great discomfort, from the south gate of the Taj Mahal to the tomb itself, a distance of about three hundred yards. It must have seemed like five miles to him. I offered him a wheelchair, but he refused. It had been his life's ambition to get to this modern wonder of the world, and he was going to do it on his own two feet. He did.

This spirit radiates from so many elderly and disabled passengers. I particularly recall Muriel and Elsie, who had been friends from childhood. Neither had ever married, and both had been fortunate to have inherited enough money to live comfortably and travel widely. Muriel, at eighty-three, was the younger of the two, short in stature, broad in beam. Elsie, eighty-six, was thin, taller than Muriel, and very much the boss of the partnership. Muriel had bad legs and, when walking, was usually found leaning heavily on her companion, whose taller frame stooped to help her as she walked around the swaying ship. However, on stable land, she walked with a cane and needed help only on difficult terrain.

We had arrived in Kobe. This was our last call in Japan before crossing to the Hawaiian Islands. This port gave us access to Tokyo, for which we had arranged an excellent tour. All tours have an escort supplied by the land tour operator. An escort is habitually there to look after any problems, to make sure everybody is back on the bus, and, generally, to care for the passengers. However, on many tours, especially long overlands, I have always made sure that a responsible member of the staff or crew is present as an escort. I have seldom found time to enjoy tours myself in this way. Nevertheless, I had decided to go on this tour as an escort, where I found myself, quite by chance, responsible for the same bus in which Muriel and Elsie were traveling. It is always wise, but not necessarily popular, to put people with a walking disability in the front seats. Because both of them were popular and befriended by many passengers, the decision was welcomed.

We made several stops along the route, visiting temples, pagodas, exotic gardens, etc., and I always went first to see whether the passengers with walking disabilities had to face a great number of steps. If the going was not good, they would stay on the coach, and, for them, I would try to get some literature or a postcard. No matter what problems had to be faced, Muriel was always first off the bus.

We arrived at the Imperial Hotel for lunch. And what a day to arrive. The lobby was full of the most beautiful Japanese girls. Today was their graduation, and, dressed in their gorgeous kimonos, they made a sight that, I am sure, no one will ever forget.

We made our way to the seventh floor of this magnificent hotel, where our lunch was laid out buffet style and a sensible mix of American and Japanese fare. After lunch, I made a short speech on what we were going to do during the afternoon and told them to gather outside in the car park opposite the main door of the hotel. I gave them thirty minutes to make a visit to the restrooms situated on the same floor, to shop, and to see if the girls were still around, and, if they were, to save one for me!

At the end of the allotted time, I stood in the car park to count my flock. Everyone was there except Muriel and Elsie. I quickly made my way back into the hotel. The first person I met was Elsie, who was walking toward me in an agitated fashion. She had lost Muriel. Apparently, Muriel had left after lunch for the restroom without requiring Elsie's help. But Muriel was no longer there. The Imperial is a large hotel, so

I decided to ask the front desk personnel about the restrooms and where they were located. They were very helpful. A member of the staff accompanied both Elsie and me on a grand tour of the hotel and the restrooms.

We reached the ninth floor, and Elsie was directed to a restroom by the young man.

"Muriel, are you here?" called Elsie.

The call was met with a reply in the affirmative.

"Thank God!" I whispered under my breath. However, the next sound I heard was peals of laughter from Muriel. Elsie reappeared with a strange expression on her face. "She's stuck!" she said.

"Where's she stuck?" I cried.

"In the toilet," Elsie replied.

Now, at this point, I must mention to the lesser-traveled that there are two forms of toilet fittings in Japan, one for them and one for us. Muriel was held by the one for them. To be brief, you do not sit, you squat. There is an imprint for both feet to give you a better chance of staying upright during the performance. Muriel had missed the imprints and was now reclining on her back, feet in the air, snugly caught in the toilet hole.

Elsie was in no state to lift her out, and Muriel was still laughing as I entered her "resting place." I laughed with her, as I got her up from the toilet. Being very British and showing no embarrassment, I said that we must be going, as the passengers were waiting for us.

"But I haven't *been* yet!" she exclaimed.

What I did next was beyond the call for an escort or for a cruise director either, for that matter. Suffice it to say, Muriel was going to be okay for the long drive back to Kobe. It was unlikely that she would entertain the thought, or indeed have the need, for another "Oriental pit stop."

For the remaining fifteen days of the cruise, whenever

Muriel's eyes met mine, a deeper understanding of life and travel was kindled.

Grandmas at Sea

When I was a young boy, I visited my grandparents every Sunday. They had lived in the same terraced house in north London for most of their lives. My grandmother was slow-moving and always seemed to be sighing. My grandfather never went anywhere and just sat by the fire smoking his pipe. He seemed to have no interest in anything other than the morning and evening newspapers. Granddad was sixty years of age, considered very old and past it in those days. What a difference today. The irrepressible energy of so-called old people bears no relation to the elderly of generations ago. Age does not weary them, nor the years condemn.

In honor of these people, most of whom are grandmas, we always have a tea or sherry party, which the grandfathers can also attend, subject to their behaving themselves. We give prizes for the oldest, the youngest, the one with the most grandchildren and photographs of the little darlings. It's a fun affair, featuring a finale consisting of their favorite stories about their grandchildren, and over the years, the grandmas have regaled us with many very funny stories. I thought I might share some with you.

The first is about a little girl who kept taking her mother's perfume. She would be told repeatedly not to touch it. One day the grandchild, who was eight years old, turned up at the drugstore where her grandma worked as a part-time cashier. She did not see her grandma as she made her way to the perfume counter, where she asked the assistant for a bottle of perfume.

"Do you want to give it as a present to your mummy?" the assistant inquired.

"No," she replied, "it's for me."

Smiling, the assistant asked the little girl what brand she wanted.

"I don't know," she said. "What have you got?"

The assistant listed what she could offer. "We have Poison, Jealousy, Love in the Mist, Desire, Passion, and . . . "

At this point, the youngster interrupted and, looking up quizzically at the assistant, said, "Do you have anything for a beginner?"

Another one that gets a good laugh is the grandson who proudly came home and told his grandma that he had been voted the friendliest boy in the school. He was to receive his prize on speech day when all the parents would be present. The day arrived, and the moment came when he was given the award by the headmaster. After presenting it, he asked the boy if he wished to say something. The grandson turned to the audience, which consisted of classmates and parents. "Thank you for giving me this prize for being the friendliest boy in the school. It was not easy to win because most of you aren't very nice."

Although there are many more, this next one is my favorite. Grandma had taken her seven-year-old granddaughter to the doctor's for a reason I cannot remember. In the waiting room sat a very large middle-aged lady. She had to weigh at least three hundred pounds. The grandchild sat on her grandma's right and this lady on her grandma's left. The child had never seen a woman this size before and, fascinated by her, constantly peeked around her grandma at the woman. Grandma continually pulled her back, telling her it was rude to stare. Then Grandma started to read a magazine when the child once again looked around, pointed at the woman's tummy, and said, "Have you got babies in there?"

The grandma pulled the child back and scolded her, whilst the woman, turning her head away in disgust, said indignantly, "No, I have not."

The waiting room went silent. The young child, head down and hurt, still had something on her mind.

Her grandma was once again absorbed in her magazine when the granddaughter looked around once more and said to the woman, "If you would like a baby in there, I know my daddy could help you."

I have no record of what response the granddaughter's remark brought.

So you see why we always look forward to entertaining the grandmas and to their entertaining us with things children say in innocence that grownups could never get away with.

Some Ups and Downs of Cruising

On departure days, many things can go wrong: loading problems, lack of supplies, late passengers, and so on. But one particular season in New York, we experienced something quite new.

Our elevators were manned by young boys, most of them Irish. The average age was sixteen, and the sap had started to rise. These cruises to the Caribbean attracted a lot of young people, among them many teenage girls. The charm of the Irish, plus the romantic Caribbean nights, swept many a young lass off her feet.

The ship had docked in New York in February. It was now May, and spring had arrived. Seeds that had been sown in winter were showing signs of blooming, and I don't mean in the parks. Some of the girls who had sailed to the Caribbean had collected more than a suntan. Parents and big brothers were not happy. Their daughters and sisters, having confessed to where the seed had been planted, created a problem the staff captain had never thought he would have to deal with. Angry parents started to appear at the gangway looking for should-be fathers, most of whom were named Patrick.

On this particular sailing day, I happened to be passing the top of the gangway when a very large man approached me. Beside him was a young, buxom girl, who, I assumed, was his daughter, her head bowed as if in prayer. The man asked me if I knew a crew member by the name of Patrick.

"There are many," I said.

"This one has red hair," he stated.

"Quite a few have," I replied.

I suggested he speak with the crew purser. I walked along the deck and showed him into the purser's foyer. Thanking me, he made his way over to the desk, with his charge looking even more dejected. (I found out later that he was not her father but her big brother.) The purser, not realizing the situation, had provided information the girl was not prepared to give, namely, what this particular Patrick did and where he could be found.

This Patrick was working the forward elevator that afternoon. It did not take them long to find him. They were on the sun deck when the doors of the elevator opened. Patrick's Irish eyes ceased to smile when he saw the face of his romantic interlude of some ten weeks before. After a nod of recognition, the battle commenced. Patrick, not having his shillelagh with him, did not fare well. He was rescued by some of the crew and taken to the hospital. The big brother was seen by the staff captain, then escorted from the ship by two New York policemen of Irish descent.

On our very next call to New York, another incident occurred. The master at arms was on duty at the bottom of the gangway when a mother and young daughter arrived, asking if they could see the ship. He said they could come on board only if they knew one of the passengers or crew. The mother said her daughter knew an elevator boy named Patrick. The master of arms, fully aware of the previous caller's problem, asked her if there was something she might like to talk to the staff captain about. The mother, realizing that he had an idea of what it was all about, agreed to see the captain. I never knew exactly what transpired at that meeting; suffice to say that Patrick was sent home to increase the birthrate in his own country. By this time, other crew members bearing the name of Patrick were seriously considering changing their names.

It was fortunate for Patrick that he had been sent home, for another irate father appeared on the gangway, trying to force his way onto the ship, only to be followed in the next several weeks by more fathers, more big brothers, sometimes with priests and ministers in their wake. They could not accept Patrick's return to the Emerald Isle. The New York police were now treating fortnightly visits to us as a standing order.

October arrived and it was time to leave New York for Southampton. As we pulled away from the dock, many well-wishers and friends were there to say good-bye, including several New York policemen. I am sure they will always keep a place in their hearts for the Irish elevator boy whose life on board certainly had its ups and downs, in more ways than one. The IRA (Irish Reproduction Association), New York branch, over which Patrick had so ably presided, was now sadly disbanded.

In a memorable season, during which we had gone aground twice (once in Grenada and once in Saint Thomas), the main shaft had seized up off Martinique when we were doing twenty-five knots, the overnight air-conditioning had expired (of course, on the hottest night on record in New York) and most of the crew had slept on deck, we all agreed the thing we would remember most was the specter of prowling parents, grimly seeking to redeem the family honor and lying in wait for unsuspecting seamen.

Just like the Movies

November 1978

I made it at last, my long-awaited visit to Egypt. I decided to escort the tour of one hundred passengers for our overnight stay in Cairo. We drove from Alexandria down to the Mena Oberi Hotel, lying in the shadow of the pyramids. I was given a magnificent suite with a balcony. After a long day sightseeing in Cairo, we came back to the hotel, where I showered and changed for dinner. I sat on my balcony to enjoy the view.

Silhouetted against a starry sky, five camels and their riders silently made their way across the top of sandy ridge. Ahead of them, bathed in moonlight, stood the great pyramid of Cheops. I was transported back thousands of years, looking at a scene that has never changed.

From the next balcony, divided from mine by an Arabic fret screen, I heard a man's voice uttering words that I had just been thinking. I walked to the balustrade and leaned over. Looking over his balcony was my neighbor. The voice I had heard, and the face I could now see, came together. It belonged to Omar Sharif.

I apologized for my intrusion and once again commented on the great view. He was very friendly and inquired what I was doing in Cairo. I told him I was a cruise director escorting a Royal Viking tour. Those dark eyes of his lit up as he mentioned that some of his bridge friends had sailed with us and had said how much they enjoyed it. I asked him what brought him to Cairo. He replied he was making a documentary film on the pyramids. I mentioned we were going to see them tomorrow. We wished each other "Bon appetit." Finishing my drink, I went down to dinner. I couldn't wait to tell the ladies in my party whom I had just met.

On arriving in the dining room, I went around my group's reserved tables to say hello. They were happily surprised to hear who my neighbor was and hoped that he was going to dine in the hotel. With only one door into the dining room, their attention to their food vied with their attention to that one entrance.

Fortunately, Omar did come down, but as he stepped into the dining room, all the lights went out. Usually, lighting works the other way when a star makes an entrance; but this was Cairo, and power failures have to be expected at the wrong time. A sigh of disappointment went up from everyone in the room, but for my group it had added feeling, as Omar had vanished in the blackout. Candles were quickly lit, giving the scene a romantic atmosphere.

As candlelight filled the room, we saw Omar being shown to a table in our section. As he was being seated, I caught his eye. I stood up and swept my hand over the group. He smiled and waved in recognition. Every face lit up as each one smiled and waved back. I knew whatever might happen, for the ladies especially, this was going to be a highlight. On returning home, they could truthfully say they had spent a romantic evening having dinner by candlelight, in the shadow of the pyramids, with Omar Sharif.

Now, what could be better that?

Rich and Famous I

During my twelve years as a cruise director with the Royal Viking Line, I was surrounded by what is euphemistically known as the "rich and famous." Of course, one could not be poor to sail this elegant line and not all were famous, but they all were interesting and became very much a part of the Royal Viking family.

I am frequently asked to talk about the many famous people we entertained on board. Most film stars and celebrities we carried have been written about many times, so I made it a habit never to question them about their private lives. The only time I did this was in a "Mann Interview" program for the passengers, where we would go over all the questions beforehand.

On one occasion, I did involve a star with an open question-and-answer session. This came about after a chat about the *National Inquirer*. I mentioned to my guest that such a newspaper could be put out of business if the stars were to produce their own, revealing all, and leaving nothing for anyone else to talk about. Imagine my surprise when my superstar guest for the 1983 world cruise said he would love to do an open question-and-answer session.

"Now hold on," I said. "With the life and the wives you have had, you would be putting your head in the lion's mouth. I really don't think it would be wise, especially with your fifth wife sitting in the front row!" He was adamant we should do it. So we programmed this very special event for later in the cruise.

Our theater was packed. Standing room only! We had decided to use a film that he had brought along, featuring Frank Sinatra (a very close friend of his) presenting our distinguished guest with with an Oscar. The film opened with Sinatra at his most eloquent introducing the recipient.

When he mentioned the name, our star walked on in front of his image on the screen and started to talk to the passengers about the film industry. His description of a scene and the details that had to be considered in its shooting were fascinating. After some twenty minutes' talking about his art, he asked the passengers if they would like to ask questions. He was insistent that they ask whatever they wished and not be embarrassed. The questions were all rather mild, and as my assistant put it, "rather RVL" (Royal Viking Line).

After it was over, I went up with him to his penthouse suite for a nightcap.

"Well," I said, "I couldn't have been more wrong about that if I had tried."

"Never mind," he replied. "Next week we'll do it for the crew, and then you'll be right."

We did, and I was. After the talk on filming, he asked for questions, and with that, he got the lot. It was fascinating to see the way he answered some of the most intimate questions such as, "How much money do you have?"

"I'm not really sure. I am always too busy to count it—probably in excess of twenty million."

"Which one of your wives was the best lover?"

"You're looking at her." (His wife, Barbara, was sitting beside him!)

"Did you have an affair with Sophia Loren?"

"Wouldn't you?"

"Have you anything left in life you want to do?"

"Yes," Cary Grant replied, "beat Derek Mann at backgammon."

In all the years I have cruised, I have never seen so many people at a gangway to greet a film star who was sailing with us. Cary Grant's fame had no bounds. In every one of the twenty countries we visited, his fans were on the pier to greet him.

Early in the cruise, I asked Cary and his bride at which of the twenty-three ports we were visiting could we have the pleasure of entertaining them both for the day. They chose Cape Town, which happened to be one of our favorite places.

The night before we arrived in Cape Town, I went to the purser and got a few hundred dollars. A few days before that, I had contacted our agent and arranged for a VIP driver and a limousine suitable for Mr. and Mrs. Cary Grant and his entourage.

The morning of our arrival was magnificent. Table Mountain could not have been clearer, and the sun was fanned by a cool breeze from the Atlantic. I was leaving the ship in the capable hands of my assistant and went to the drawer of my desk to get the money. It was gone. No one had ever stolen money on our ship before.

I went back to the reception and collected more money, telling the chief purser quietly what had happened. I did not know Cary was behind me, listening to what was going on. He interrupted me and said, in effect, no way was I going to take them out. He was quite upset and was shocked at my losing that amount. He wanted to call the whole day off. However, I made light of it, and after a few moments, we left for Table Mountain.

I had asked the agent to arrange for us to take a cable up before it was properly opened for the public. And so it was that we arrived early at the base of the railhead and made our way to the little booking booth. After paying our fare, we moved to an area where we saw an Indian boy dressed neatly in a white shirt and nicely pressed trousers. He had been waiting for the cable railway to officially open, and I asked Cary if he would mind if the boy accompanied us. Cary was happy for him to join us, and the boy did.

At this point, I must remind you that Cary was seventy-nine years old and had not made a film in twenty years. He worked very hard at maintaining his privacy and avoiding television, except, of course, for his films.

I asked the youngster his name and inquired where he lived. I cannot remember his name, but he lived in New Delhi and was fourteen years old. The boy seemed a little uncomfortable, and I assumed it was because of the frightening experience of coming very close to the cliff face to climb the last section. His nervousness increased as he took from his trousers a piece of paper and a pencil, saying to Cary, "Mr. Grant, may I please have your autograph?"

I looked at my wife, Barbara, in disbelief. We had just witnessed the true meaning of the word *fame*.

There is a sequel to this story.

Rich and Famous II

A year later, we left the *Royal Viking Sky*, I resumed my position as cruise director on my favorite of the three Viking ships, the *Star*. I was cleaning out my desk on the *Sky* when I noticed a brown cash envelope jammed behind the top drawer. I reached in and found it contained the money I had lost in Cape Town. The memories of that day came flooding back. As I looked at the calendar, I saw to my surprise that it had been exactly one year ago when we were in Cape Town enjoying that unforgettable day.

During that day, we took many photographs with Cary and his beautiful wife, Barbara. On our arrival in Rio de Janeiro, I took two rolls of film to the Kodak office. The next day, I called to collect them. Not one roll had come out. Every frame was a blank. There seemed to be no explanation. It was one of the most disappointing moments of my life. However, nothing can ever take away the wonderful memories we have of that day in Cape Town with one of the most gracious and certainly one of the most charismatic men ever to grace the movie screen.

Man Over-Bored

It was early May 1972, when I sailed on the *Orcades* out of Southampton. The ship was one of nine in the prestigious P&O fleet. Built in 1948, it had seen service all over the world, but its sailing days were now numbered. Scheduled to be broken up next year, the ship was still a gracious vessel, which, with gentle care, would see a few more nautical miles before that fateful day.

This was the first of many cruises to the Mediterranean that summer. We left in torrential rain and sailed down the Solent. The shoreline was hardly visible as we sailed out into the English Channel. During the night, we left that historic piece of water to enter the Atlantic and the Bay of Biscay.

The bay has quite a history for storms and high seas. It was not long before that body of water made good its reputation. The wind increased, as did the height of the waves. Soon we were in a force-eight gale. The wind coming from the southwest reduced our speed and the passengers' appetites. The morning dawned with high seas and heavy rain. The entertainment department got cracking with additional indoor activities for those who were not lying in their cabins. By afternoon, the swells increased as did the seasickness.

By tradition, the captain's welcome cocktail party is held on the second night out. The *Orcades* was a two-class ship. Both first and second class had two sittings for dinner; therefore, the captain had a busy evening with four parties to host. I hasten to add that the entertainers also had to do four shows a night when scheduled.

There was one day more at sea before reaching our first

port, Vigo, in Spain. This day was no better than the last. Passengers were getting very weary of the motion and looking forward to getting their feet on terra firma. The captain's dinner the night before had not been a success. There were many complaints about the food being cold, the vegetables not well cooked, etc., etc. We did have a new chef on board and, linked with bad weather, cooking was not easy in the galley.

The hostess was desperately trying to keep the passengers happy with exciting things to make out of gingham, this being her forte. Bingo and horseracing (the game) occupied a great deal of the time, as well as arm exercises in the bars.

With relief, we arrived in Vigo, which lies one hundred miles north of Portugal. It had been attacked in 1585 by Sir Francis Drake, and after that, it seemed content to become a fishing port. Brandy and leather are produced and sold at extremely reasonable prices, as are all alcoholic beverages. Shops, bars, and cafés are plentiful, which was a blessing, as it rained for most of the day.

We sailed at 5:00 P.M. and made our way south along the coastline of Portugal. This stretch of water was enjoying the full force of some fine Atlantic swells, doubtless the backlog of the storm. Another day of bingo, horseracing, indoor games, and, yes, gingham. Two of the artists had succumbed to seasickness, which meant that previous acts were, of necessity, encored—hardly variety! One of the projectors in the cinema gave up the ghost, and both the bridge and port lecturers were indisposed.

We had two days at sea before our next port. Soon we were to enter the Mediterranean through the Strait of Gibraltar. Here, we hoped the weather would improve, but, to worsen matters, the hostess was running out of gingham. If that happened, we would doubtless have a mutiny.

On rare occasions bad weather can continue for many

days. It is then that a cruise director and his staff have to do their best to keep people occupied in suitable activities, mainly those that involve sitting down. With only one cinema projector working, the passengers were getting fed up with the operator's taking twenty minutes to rewind the spools.

Complaints were coming in about the smell of sewage. Because of so much motion, in more ways than one, the old ship's pipes were showing problems. The first pipe burst in the second-class section; then, showing no class distinction, one burst in the first. A problem was now developing of a more serious nature, diarrhea. Passengers are fed and watered every two hours, and their tummies are not used to it. Also, people are inclined to drink more alcohol. With the bad weather, quite a few were dehydrated and their level of resistance lowered. Though it did not get to serious proportions, it was something else to "gripe" about.

The next day dawned with the sun shining in a cloudless sky. Although the sea had calmed down, there was a strong wind. The captain had roped off the forward area of the promenade deck to prevent accidents. I decided to get some air on the very top deck. As I walked out, there was a lady passenger with the same idea. Suddenly, there was a very strong gust of wind that blew us off balance. She grabbed onto me as the force of the wind took us both like tumbleweed from one end of the deck to the other. We crashed into the bulkhead at the aft end. I was bruised, but there were no broken bones. I had taken the full force, but my new-found friend was unscathed. We were both shaken and we sat for a time with our backs to the bulkhead, getting our breath and composure back.

After a few minutes, we made it inside, she going to her cabin and I taking my aching body to the forward lounge. Sitting by the window was my partner, who could see I was uncomfortable. As I told him my story, someone flew past the window.

"Oh, my God!" I exclaimed, "that was a body."

My partner leaned back in his chair and nonchalantly replied, "Well, somebody's got the right idea."

The ship started to make a full turn to port, as we ran out onto the promenade deck. Obviously, someone had seen the body go overboard and raised the alarm. A ship is navigated to form a figure eight when somebody leaves it other than by the gangway. This allows a full viewing of the previous course.

We could see the victim in the distance over the starboard side. By now all the passengers had rushed to the rail. This was the first piece of excitement they had had on a rather boring cruise. The accident boat had been lowered and was making its way toward him. He was lying on a lifebelt, which somebody had kindly thrown, and was swimming slowly, but surely, back to the ship.

When he was about two hundred yards away, a voice called out, "You shouldn't have gone that far, old chap. A letter to the chairman would have sufficed." With that, about a thousand passengers broke up in laughter, breaking the tension of the last few days.

The unlucky man overboard was a crew member. He had been painting the rail on the top deck when he fell. Fortunately, he was okay and had suffered no broken bones. In fact, he was smiling and waving as he stepped off the accident boat. This incident brought everybody together, and the ship became a happier place. By the time we got to Naples, everybody was having a good time.

At this point, one story about Naples is worth mentioning. It involved a close friend of mine, Hugh Auld, who was working as a shore excursion manager. In later years, Hugh became my assistant cruise director. There was no nicer person that you could wish to meet. He has since passed away. Not only my wife and I still miss him but all the people who ever knew him do as well.

Hugh had given a talk on the tours in Naples and said the ruins of Pompeii were one of the highlights. He mentioned that the tour was very tiring, and one must be prepared to walk for five hours, sandwiched between a long coach journey there and back.

Naples produced a warm and sunny day, with many passengers taking the tour to Pompeii. Later that afternoon, when coaches were returning from that excursion, Hugh happened to be on the dock. He walked over to welcome home his flock. Helping them off the coach, Hugh was asking how they had enjoyed their day. They all seemed to have had a good time, even though they were all rather tired.

One of the last passengers off the coach was an elderly lady. "Did you have a good day?" inquired Hugh.

"No, I didn't. It was very tiring," she said, in an agitated voice.

"Well, I did tell you that it would be a strenuous tour," he said.

"Did you know there isn't a toilet on this bus?" she exclaimed.

Hugh admitted that he did not.

"And another thing, young man. Why did they have to build those ruins so far out of town?"

At the end of the cruise, we had the usual masquerade. In those early days, we would have at least three hundred people participating. Nowadays, with so much entertainment and television, few people ever bother to dress up. This particular masquerade had two memorable winners.

The first was a man dressed completely out of next

163

year's cruise catalogs. Remembering the diarrhea, he'd entitled his costume, "next year's 'runs' on P&O."

The other was a man with a life ring around his neck. His face was made up with long dark lines and heavy circles round his eyes. His body was festooned with every gingham project the long-suffering hostess had created. He walked slowly and dejectedly across the stage. His sign read, MAN-OVER-BORED.

It may sound strange to say, but in the end, this cruise produced high ratings. The staff, officers, and crew bent over backwards to get the problems solved. It is amazing what one can do when the chips are down and the ruins so far out at sea.

Wrong Number

Sailing down the Mexican coast on her way to Acapulco, the *Royal Viking Sky* was bathed in glorious sunshine, as were its passengers. The evening bought forth a sunset worthy of travel brochures, and the night was lit with a thousand stars. The show was over in the main lounge, and the passengers were wending their way to the next venue of entertainment. They were, in most cases, retiring after an exhausting day of doing nothing or everything.

The reception desk, open twenty-four hours, had a quiet time. The passengers had become used to the ship, and the noises of the first night demanding cabin changes were behind them. They now knew the way to the dining room.

At 11:15 P.M., noted in the reception log, a call came from cabin 256. Mrs. Lambert was ringing, requesting the doctor. Her husband was complaining of severe stomach pains. As always in these situations, the nurse on duty was called by beeper to contact 256.

As she was on the top deck at the time and forward of the ship, she made her way down to the lower deck, where the hospital was located. Collecting her bag, she called the cabin to let Mr. and Mrs. Lambert know she was on her way. She dialed 256, only to find that the occupants had not called for the doctor and that all was well.

A few of the cabins on Royal Viking ships are midships and have numbers followed by the letter M. The nurse realized that the person phoning reception had forgotten to add the number 5, which indicates all midship cabins. Then she dialed the appropriate number—556—putting a five instead of the two. Mrs. Lambert answered and was a little agitated because of the delay and also because the nurse was ringing and not the doctor.

The time was now 11:30 P.M. and the nurse had diagnosed the usual problem of too much food and drink in a tummy that was only used to one martini and two small meals a day. It was, therefore, complaining in no uncertain terms to its seventy-five-year-old owner. After administering the medication, the nurse returned to the hospital. At midnight, she would go off duty, as would the receptionist, and the night watch would take over.

Just after midnight, the new receptionist noticed on the pad that there had been a call from 256. It was not possible to contact the previous receptionist to see if it had been attended to, so she rang the hospital. The nurse said that 256M had called, and that that had been dealt with. She suggested, however, that the receptionist had better ring 256 just in case there had been another call.

The passenger in 256 was obviously, by the sound of her voice, wakened from a deep sleep. She said that this was the second call and that there was nothing wrong and requested that she and her husband *please* not be disturbed again. As the disgruntled passenger put down the phone, she noticed that the covers had slid off her husband, and so she pulled them over his back.

Something was wrong; he was too still. She moved him over onto his back. His eyes were staring. He was not breathing. He was dead. Estimated time of death, 11:15 P.M.—the time of the first call from 256M.

Burial at Sea

Many cruise ships can carry a thousand passengers or more. Add to this a crew of over 50 percent of the passenger load, and you have the population of a small town. Cruise ships are not associated with death, but it happens. This is especially true when it comes to long cruises, and the age group is high. On my first world cruise, I was travelling on a ship that actually carried 1,600 passengers and 800 crew! On that voyage of one hundred days, we lost twenty passengers and one crew member through suicide.

The strangest was the first. He was a Scottish peer of the realm. He came to the purser's office the day before our arrival in Lisbon and inquired after the exchange rate of the escudo to the pound. When told the amount, he uttered a cry and dropped dead. The Scots are known for taking financial matters seriously, but we all felt that this was a bit excessive.

In days gone by, many ships buried the dead at sea, subject to death being from natural causes. Any questionable passing of a person on board has to be reported and investigated by the police, usually at the next port. However, when circumstances allow, and permission is given by the next of kin, either traveling on board or contacted on shore, burial at sea is the normal practice. Today, with the many restrictions imposed on ships as regards anything being dumped overboard, plus other legal ramifications, burial at sea has become rare. The cost of transporting a body by air involves a great deal of red tape and considerable expense, but in my experience, most Americans prefer to transport the body back to the States.

However, on occasion passengers bring an urn on board containing the ashes of a loved one to be scattered on waters requested by the deceased. Even a simple procedure like this can go wrong. Billy McComb, probably one of the most respected and entertaining magicians of our time, had been requested in the will of his friend, a fellow member of the art, to scatter his ashes at sea. Billy had sailed with me many times and was frequently employed by leasing cruise lines, so the request posed no problems. This was until the ceremony.

Billy decided it should be attended by the captain and other uniformed members of the ship's company. They assembled on the fantail, and, after a few words, which Billy never has much difficulty in finding, he scattered the ashes over the side. Unfortunately, at that very moment, the wind shifted and the ashes of the dearly departed returned onboard, all over the white uniforms of those in attendance. It was not the moving, magical moment Billy had hoped for.

On one occasion, we were sailing in the Mediterranean, when an American gentleman passed away. His wife was traveling with him.

He had been ill for some time, finally succumbing to a heart attack. Our next port was two days away, and I was trying to persuade her to let us bury him at sea.

The port to which we were sailing had been the cause of problems two years earlier for an American family when their grandfather passed away on board, and we had to land the body there. We had told the eldest son that, if he wished, we could bury his father at sea. However, the family had decided to take him home to the United States.

I continued to tell the bereaved passenger that, many months later, I had received a letter from the son, who told me how much he had regretted not taking our advice in having his father buried at sea. It had taken three days to get his father's body out of the country. The police had demanded an autopsy, the authorities had made their lives hell, and, only after getting the American ambassador personally involved, had they managed to get the body back home to the United States. It had cost nine thousand dollars!

After listening to my story, a determined face looked me straight in the eye and said, "He's going home no matter what the cost. I ain't going to waste that plot of land we bought in 1935, and I'm certainly not going to spend eternity sleeping alone."

The burial service at sea, is short, dignified, and conducted at sunrise. A platform is set up in the gangway exit closest to the waterline, the end of it sloping toward the exit. The coffin rests on the platform and is covered with a black cloth.

One end of the coffin has a flap for the body to pass through and is operated by a lever. The body is weighted at the feet, allowing it to slip easily into the sea and to slide down to the ocean bed. In the days of sail, it was the job of the sailmaker to sew the body into a sailcloth bag. The last stitch was always through the lower part of the nose. This was to ensure that the deceased was definitely deceased. Fortunately, today, we have a doctor on board to make this practice unnecessary.

This particular burial at sea happened on a Mediterranean cruise over twenty years ago. An elderly couple was seated at my table. The wife mentioned to me that her husband had suffered from heart trouble and probably did not have long to live. Unfortunately, she was right; he died on the sixth day out. She wished for him to be buried at sea. As he'd died of natural causes, there were no problems. The service was arranged to take place as we passed the island of Malta, which had been their favorite holiday place throughout the years.

I had nothing to do with the service. However, as they had been seated at my table, I felt I should attend. I arose early that morning and, after putting on a dark suit, made my way to the lower gangway area. Just after 5:00 A.M., four sailors and the bos'n arrived with the coffin. They laid it on the platform and covered it with a black cloth. The housekeeper had arranged for a wreath to be put on top, and all was ready for 5:30 A.M.

The bos'n was instructing one of the seamen how to operate the lever and said, "When the captain says, 'We commit his body to the deep,' *then* you pull the lever." So the sailor pulled the lever, and with that, the body left the ship prematurely and disappeared into the Mediterranean.

Because he was of another nationality, the poor sailor had mistaken the "then" for "now." The bos'n's face was a study, and the language that ensued from his lips was, to say the least, colorful. I didn't know whether to laugh or cry. Quick thinking was the order of the day. *Something had to replace the body!* After a few moments of serious thought, I had the answer. It lay in the library.

The first thing was to stop the captain and the bereaved wife from coming at 5:50 A.M. I rang the captain, telling him there would be a delay. Fortunately, he did not ask why, and I told him that we would ring him when everything was set. Meanwhile, an able seaman was letting the bereaved know about a slight delay.

The bos'n had left to get another body bag from the hospital, while I made my way to the library. The day before I had been helping clear out old and damaged books. These were to be replaced by new ones in the hold. Another body bag was delivered to me in the library, and it was then that I realized we needed something to give it shape. I remembered the cardboard sheets we used in the gangway areas. I sent the seaman to find some. On his return, I rolled up the cardboard sheet, placed it in the bag, and filled the rolled sheet with the heaviest books.

The bos'n arrived with two sailors to see how we were doing, almost asking, "Is it a body yet?" By now, it was 5:30 A.M., and we still had some ways to go. After zipping up the bag, we realized that we had no lead weight for the bottom. The bos'n ran off to find the duty engineer for some lead. This took time, but, eventually, the "bookman" was in place inside the coffin on the platform.

The duty officer called the captain, and an able seaman was sent to bring the widow of the deceased. They arrived together, and the service was conducted with dignity and a lot of self-control by those who knew the contents of the bag. We decided not to tell the captain till afterwards and, certainly, never the widow. This time the bos'n pulled the lever.

In the ship's log, the entry read: "The body left the ship at 5:55 A.M." It did not say it left in a novel fashion, but things don't always go by the book at sea!

Wave Me Nearly Good-bye

Here is a report I sent in 1991 from the *Regent Sea* after experiencing a storm in the Gulf of Alaska. Storms in that area are unusual before late September, when all the cruise ships have gone south. But this one arrived early in September, as we were leaving.

The passengers boarded in driving rain and a high tide, making the gangway comparable to climbing the Matterhorn. The next morning saw threatening skies, and, by midday, as we were leaving Prince William Sound, the ship started to move in an unpredictable manner. The wind increased on our port side and the swell, directly on the prow. By midafternoon, the seas had increased to thirty feet, and the wind velocity to seventy-five knots. Passengers with cabins in the forward part of the ship could not take the movement and slept in the midship lounges. Many were seasick, and the infirmary was overwhelmed with calls. We canceled the captain's cocktail party, the first time I have ever done that in twenty years. The television set in my cabin left the table, bounced on the floor, and landed beside me on the couch. [It still works, by God!] Out of 720 passengers, only 40 hardy souls came down to dinner.

With good seamanship by the captain, and a well-built ship drawing twenty-nine feet, she rode the storm well, considering its severity.

Other vessels around us did not fare so well, however.

As nerve-wracking as that was, that Alaska storm was nothing in comparison to another I experienced. In my twenty years at sea and sailing over one million sea miles, I have only been through six big storms and have been truly frightened only once. Other rough seas may have been bad and may have provided some exciting moments, but this one was different.

We were in the North Atlantic, sailing on the *Canberra* to Southampton out of New York. Winter was settling in, and the wind was blowing fiercely. Very soon, we were to experience a North Atlantic roller, enormous waves that are more like huge swells. Many of these originate from the Davis

Strait, which lies between Newfoundland and Greenland. Massive falls of ice and high winds coming from the Arctic create these monsters. When they come on the ship's side rather than the front, you get the full effect of their severity.*

This particular wave came just after dinner as we were enjoying a brandy in the Crow's Nest Bar, high up forward on the ship. As we sipped our drinks, I began to feel an odd sensation, as if the ship were being lifted up. A creaking sound heralded a movement unlike anything I had ever experienced. Very slowly, the ship started to heel over.

My drink slid across the table. I managed to grab it before it slipped off. The sound of crashing glass and bottles merely signaled the sound of heavier items in the ship suddenly set adrift. My chair was no longer interested ln supporting me, as it moved over on two legs. I was required to put out my free hand (the other still holding the drink) to balance myself. The ship was continuing to keel over, as the chair slid out from under me.

I was forced to drop the glass so that I could kneel on the floor. Everything in the room was now in motion toward the port side. Scenes from the *Poseidon Adventure* flashed into my mind. Cries and screams joined the sound of things crashing against the bulkhead. The slowness of the movement, seemingly never ending, made it all the more terrifying. When was it going to stop? The ship seemed to be taking one last deep breath before going over to an angle from which there could be no return.

---

*The *Queen Mary* has encountered these waves many times. On one occasion, a cook on board told me that the *Mary* drove hard into a roller before riding it. He saw one of the huge lateral girders that strengthened the ship bend slightly under the pressure of water on the prow. The paint covering it started to flake off and fell into the soup he was cooking.

Suddenly, it stopped and very slowly the ship made its way back to the perpendicular. Cries of fear were replaced by sighs of relief, joining the sound of glass and equipment making its way back from whence it came.

However, we failed to realize the ship had to go down the other side of this enormous wave. Everything began to happen now in reverse. So back again we went, but this time, mercifully, the ship only tilted a few degrees before it finally righted itself. We had survived. Now everybody was talking. The most-used phrase I can remember was, "What are you having?" The problem now was that most of the bottles were broken.

Better those departed spirits than ourselves.

UFOs

The Skald Club was created by the Royal Viking Line for its repeat passengers. The repeat passenger is the backbone of any successful cruise line. At the end of my tenure with the company, it was not unusual to have a good 60 percent as repeaters on a cruise. However, on special Skald cruises we could have as many as 90 percent. These cruises were often hosted by famous people.

In April 1977, we were privileged to have one of the original team of the seven astronauts, Gordon Cooper, accompanied by his charming wife, Susan. Gordon made the last Mercury flight in 1963, circling the earth twenty-two times. At the end of the flight, the automatic control system broke down, and he piloted the craft manually, landing only five miles from the primary recovery ship. This was a remarkable feat so early in the space program.

We were sailing the Mediterranean for forty-five days, and on our call in Israel, Gordon was given the VIP treatment.

He kindly invited six of us to join him. It turned out to be the two most exciting days I have ever spent in a foreign land. Our guide was a professor of history, who brought the Old and New Testament stories to life at the various sites we visited. I remember at one point we stopped at a small village. He walked us over to the square, where, in the center, there was a well. He verbally created a picture for us of what life would have been like in the village at the time of Christ. We felt transported back to those times, so colorful and real was his description. Suddenly, he paused and, pointing to where we stood, said, "And it was where you stand—Christ restored the sight of the blind man." It is impossible to describe the emotion I felt at that moment.

For my show, "The Mann Interviews," where I chat with interesting passengers traveling with us, I chose Gordon as my special guest. I asked him a question often asked of astronauts, "Have you ever seen a UFO while up in space?" Gordon gave the same answer all have given, "No." However, he qualified this answer by saying he *had* seen UFO's in the early fifties while in Germany, where he was serving as a colonel in the U.S. Air Force. At that time, he was the leader of their famous fighter acrobatic team. He cited an amazing incident.

His team had just landed from practicing their display. Sitting outside the mess, they suddenly saw objects moving at great speed high in the sky. They watched in astonishment as the objects started to copy the exact maneuvers they had been performing.

The next day the same thing happened. Gordon rushed back to his aircraft and took off to get a closer look. He climbed in excess of fifty thousand feet, but they were still high above him. Even with his binoculars, he could not get a clear picture of their shape. He reckoned they were moving at a speed faster than anything humanly possible.

When NASA in the early sixties was still deciding the manner in which the astronauts were to be recovered, they were testing a dry landing, which was favored by the Russians. These tests were being carried out in the Nevada desert. As the parachutes came down with the space capsule, a UFO appeared and followed it, landing only a mile away from where the capsule landed. This was all filmed. Many very important people viewed the incident and, later, the film. Gordon personally flew the film back to Washington in his own plane—all this coming from one of America's most credible people.

After this remarkable interview, we went back to my office. A knock came at the door, and in came a lady who was in quite an emotional state. She told us of an experience she had had with a UFO many years before. She was a rancher's wife, and one day in her kitchen she saw a dazzling light come down toward their woods, some four hundred yards from the house. She made her way out into the yard and started to walk toward the object, which had by then settled in the woods. As she got nearer, the heat became intense. The light was so bright she could not look straight at it. Without warning, the object started to rise and, after climbing a hundred feet off the ground, accelerated upwards at tremendous speed. Moving towards where it had landed, she observed that the area was flattened and charred.

Her first thought was to phone the police, but she decided to wait until her husband came home to tell him. He just did not believe her and told her she had imagined it all. He forbade her to phone the police, telling her to forget it. From that day on she had been laboring under the misapprehension that she was slightly batty. So now, hearing of Gordon's experiences from the astronaut himself a great weight had been lifted from her shoulders.

As Susan and Gordon left the ship, Susan told us how

much they had enjoyed everything, but also how close she had been to not coming. Gordon had been asked by the World UFO Society to be the main speaker at their international conference in Mexico at the Acapulco Princess. It was taking place at the same time as our cruise. Susan informed Gordon that, if he had agreed to go and had missed the cruise, she would have thrown a few identifiable objects in his direction and would have left him for someone else's space.

It was now my turn to tell Gordon of an incident I had experienced in England one night in 1972. After returning home from a cabaret engagement, my wife and I were walking from the garage to our seventeenth-century cottage. It was a beautiful night with not a cloud in the sky. Our property was in the country, and we had an uninterrupted view for many miles. Suddenly, at about 1:00 A.M., there appeared about ten lights, very high in the sky, traveling at great speed. I thought they were a uniform formation of shooting stars. This was not the case, as they split up and shot off in different directions. After I waited a few seconds, they appeared again, back in formation, shooting across the sky. The next move had been quite frightening. As they reached a point approximately one mile above us, they turned on themselves and, in straight formation, shot back up and disappeared into the heavens.

We went into the cottage, and although it was late, I phoned the Greenwich Observatory. I got a busy signal. After half an hour, I gave up and went to bed. The next day's late papers were full of the sightings, but no explanation was given. I had not yet met Gordon, but when I told him, he said I had seen, more or less, what he and his fellow pilots had viewed in Germany some twenty years earlier.

In 1986, we were in Australia sailing out of Sydney for the Halley's comet cruises. On each cruise, our enrichment lecturers were famous physicists, among them Carl Sagan.

After listening to him and others of his ilk, it became very clear that UFOs, as we know them, are simply not possible. Nevertheless, some things just go beyond our knowledge and understanding.

Perhaps an ancestor from long ago reappearing here today and seeing a nuclear submarine emerge from the sea would literally have a heart attack from the incapacity to understand.

But consideration of the hypothesis that UFOs are airships from the future engaged in historical research forces one to ask the question, "Do we know everything?" Clearly not. Yet the discussions of UFOs and our glimpses on board ship of the unknown, the unexpected, and the intangible have been both humbling and illuminating.

Even so, it has been my privilege and my job to extend my own practical knowledge of the histories and cultures of the various ports of calls, sharing the wonders of cruising and of life at sea with all who have ventured.

Not Wanted on Voyage

In the "good old days," the great passenger ships carried thousands of immigrants across the oceans and seas to seek new lands and a new life, taking with them their life-long possessions. Much of what they carried would not be wanted on the voyage. Trunks and cases would be labeled as such and stowed away in the holds of the ships.

But there are other things that are not needed on a voyage. Labels are not attached to them, except by name. One of them is a stowaway. To be a stowaway on a ship is an offense under the Maritime Act and incurs a penalty. The penalty imposed by the law varies from country to country. In the United States there is a fine. In some other countries, it can be far more severe. In certain instances the ship itself can be heavily fined. Nevertheless, a stowaway's objective is to board a ship and remain there undetected for the duration of the voyage. The stowaway pays no fare nor works for his passage. In my experience a stowaway is successful only when aided by a member of the crew. But it's a difficult feat on one's own.

I am often asked how one can stowaway, survive, then simply walk off the ship? It would be unwise for me to propose a winning formula, but there *are* ways of doing it successfully, subject to having detailed knowledge of the surrogate home or, as mentioned, having an accomplice already on board. It would also depend on how much lead time there is for planning, as there is seldom an opportunity to case the joint or to obtain a set of plans, other than the cabin and public-room layout in a brochure.

After the hijacking of the *Achille Lauro* in the summer of 1985, security became very strict. Passenger ships now carry at least two security guards. The gangway is always manned by a watch officer, an able seaman, and, unless the ship is at anchor, a security guard. At anchor, a security guard will be on the pier as passengers board the tenders to return to the ship. Therefore, unless you have a pass, it is not easy to board as a visitor. These are issued by ship's agent or the head office of the shipping company. Most companies request forty-eight-hours' notice for a visit. In special cases, a pass can be issued on board but only if signed and approved by either the captain or the hotel manager.

I have observed a few situations involving stowaways in my time. However, all occurred before the *Achille Lauro* hijacking. The first was a dancer who came aboard the ship in Africa as part of the local entertainment. After the performance, he hid in the stage manager's storeroom behind the stage, and that was where we found him the next morning, that is, tucked away in a corner, holding a cigarette, and asking my stage manager for a light. Unfortunately, nobody in all the other African countries we were to call would take him. We had to take him all the way back to the United States and then fly him to Freetown in Sierra Leone, where he had originally boarded.

There was a similar incident aboard ship with a Fijian, who simply walked on with the local entertainment carrying a drum for his friend. He was caught the next day standing in line with the passengers at the deck lunch buffet. When asked how he had been so stupid as to eat there, he told us he could not resist the smell of the food wafting up into the fan room on the top deck. He had been there since the ship sailed. His reason for stowing was merely to be able to practice his religion. Whatever it was, it was outlawed in Fiji. He thought, being an American ship, there would have been passengers on board of the same or similar persuasion who would help him.

On another occasion, a bon voyage party guest decided that the party should not end for her, so she remained on board. Her tactics were straightforward; she appealed to the more basic instincts of the male crew members. Her first night on board was spent in the arms and bed of a bartender. She spend the next seven days and nights enjoying several members of the crew. The most difficult thing for a stowaway is to find a place to sleep and eat. She had no problem in her case; the crew looked after her in more ways than one. She managed to keep "disclothed" for seven days before she was eventually discovered by, of all people, our lady welfare officer.

When taken off the ship, our sirenic stowaway left behind not only fond memories, but a well-known sexual complaint that kept the hospital busy and gave the staff captain evidence of the guilty parties beyond all reasonable doubt.

179

A medical emergency set the stage for another incident in Los Angeles. Passengers were boarding for a Panama Canal cruise. An hour before we sailed, one of the visitors had a heart attack in the card room. We called the paramedics, and they arrived literally in minutes. No one dared stop the medical team for any formalities as they came up the gangway carrying a stretcher and life-saving equipment. An able seaman immediately took them to the card room where our nurse was giving CPR. Unfortunately, after working on the poor man for some time, they were unable to save his life.

The next morning, as we sailed down the coast of Mexico, we held our usual fire drill for the passengers. Under maritime law all passengers must attend. A gentleman was sitting alone in the Lido Bar, where service had been interrupted until after the drill. An officer passing by asked the man to go to his cabin and collect his life jacket. The man said nothing but left the bar, presumably to get the jacket.

The fire drill was in progress when a crew member noticed a man without a life jacket standing on the top deck. As luck would have it, this able seaman had escorted the medical team from the gangway to the card room and recognized the man as one of them. After the drill the seaman went to the bridge to inform the staff captain. With the captain was the officer who had spoken to the man in the Lido Bar. A search ensued, and the stowaway was found in the library, where he was apprehended without a struggle.

He told the captain he wanted to go back to Mexico. Apparently, he had had some problem with the authorities and was not allowed back into that country. He decided a good way to cross the border was to stow away on a ship. He had apparently tried before on a Princess ship but was caught before the ship had even sailed. This time he was fortunate enough to be there when the ambulance arrived and had run up the gangway with the two paramedics. It was as easy as that. We arrived in Puerto Vallarta the day after, where the local police presumably dispatched him to Los Angeles. A stowaway usually has a definite reason for leaving. It is seldom a whimsical one. Yet, oddly enough, we've come across stowaways who had no definite destination or, if they did have one, had no fixed idea on how to reach it. The latter problem was the case with a fourteen-year-old French boy who "joined" us in Amsterdam.

We were on a northern capitals cruise and had left Amsterdam on our way to the Baltic. It was summertime, and we had some children on board, most of whom were American. Children can be very clever, but few are good at keeping a secret. If they had, our little French boy might well have made his destination without detection.

He was first seen by the children at the late night buffet the day after we sailed from Amsterdam. As he was a new boy on the block, they asked him his name and where he came from. He answered them in his native tongue. Fortunately, one of the children had some school French and after a few minutes realized the situation. The children were excited and, after a vote, decided to aid him in his plight.

Apparently, he lived in central France, in the city of Lyon. He said he was very unhappy in the orphanage, where he had lived for three years following the death of his parents. Somewhere in England, he had a cousin. He was not sure where exactly, but it was near Manchester.

He had managed to escape from his group of orphans, who were on a shopping trip to a local market in the outskirts of Lyon. Seeing a motorbike parked close by, he had "borrowed" it and driven over three hundred miles north to Paris. This was some feat as his and the bike's disappearance must have been reported. Arriving in Paris, he eventually found the Gare de Nord (the northern railway station) and, leaving the bike on the curb, made his way inside to continue his journey to the coast.

Looking at the destination board, he saw Amsterdam and, remembering it was a big port, decided that was the one for him. He managed to board the train and remain undetected for the journey. He was big for his fourteen years and had the look of an educated, well-bred lad. Fortunately, dressed in his best because of the outing from the orphanage, he did not look like a lost urchin. So he did not seem to look out of place, on the train or anywhere else, come to that matter.

When he arrived in Amsterdam, he made his way out of the station and, to his relief, saw the masts of several ships in the distance. The walk to the docks from the station took him no more than twenty minutes. When eventually he got to the top of the bridge that overlooks the docks, a beautiful white cruise ship caught his eye. He decided to investigate to see where it was going.

It was a short walk through the dock to where the *Royal Viking Star* was tied up. He approached a flower seller on the dock and asked her where the ship was going. Either he misunderstood the answer, or she the question. We had just come from England, but he thought she said it was headed there. His opportunity to board the ship came when a group of five children got off a tour bus. He walked over to them, and as they started toward the gangway, he joined in behind them and walked on board.

The children managed to look after him for four days, but after that they could keep their wonderful secret no longer. Barbara was on deck doing the walkathon when one of the children, Kimberly, came and told her. Barbara felt the story was a figment of the child's imagination and played along with her.

That evening in the dining room the children marched

with the waiters and the maître d' in a parade for passengers' birthdays. After the second "Happy birthday," Kimberly pulled at Barbara's sleeve and said, "That's him." Barbara looked round and saw the boy, his pockets bulging with bread rolls he had taken from the dumbwaiters as he made his way around the dining room.

After dinner, Barbara came and told me about the boy. I got in touch with the chief purser, who, at the late night buffet, approached him, and that was that.The boy had been spending his nights in lifeboat number seven, but this night he at least would have a comfortable bed. He was tearful as the chief purser took him to the staff captain. I felt later that his tears were because the children had snitched on him and betrayed his trust, rather than at his being caught.

We had no brig (that's a ship's jail where such offenders go), but as he posed no serious threat, we kept him on the bridge of the ship, where the officer of the watch could keep an eye on him. A bed was made up in the staff captain's suite. However, we did have one problem. The next port was in Russia, and by rights he would have to be disembarked there. This would have raised many issues. We decided to keep him away from the officials, physically and on paper.

During the days the children had hid him, he had taken part in all the junior cruiser's programs. There were pictures of him in the photo gallery, enjoying the deck sports, horse racing, and other activities in which all the other kids participated.

We decided to keep the fact of our stowaway as secret as possible, no easy task on a ship comprised of 550 passengers. But the day before we arrived in Helsinki, I introduced him to all the passengers after telling his story. The passengers were captivated by it all and requested that we accept a collection for him. It amounted to over one thousand dollars.

The next morning was a tearful one as he left the ship

dressed mainly in Royal Viking logo clothing and clutching a stuffed Snoopy the children had given him. He was escorted to the French Embassy by an embassy official. The ambassador had been advised of the situation, and we had their word that every effort would be made to find his relatives and make any punishment slight.

The money collected was given to them to make reparation to the owner of the motorbike and any left over for his fare and expenses getting to England, if the search was successful. We also asked to be updated as to the progress of the search. Unfortunately, we never received any further communication and can only hope that his adventure had a happy ending. He certain had a great time on the *Star*, but who didn't under those circumstances?

Party Time or Love Me Tender

The tradition of the Bon Voyage party on cruise ships has been affected by today's tight security requirements. Passengers must apply for guest passes at least forty-eight hours before a ship sails. Gone are the nice surprises of having old friends come to cheer you on your way. The ship's departure from the dock to the cries of "Bon voyage," and "Happy sailing" are mainly a thing of the past. The Breathalyzer has not helped matters either. Cruise-ship companies have also been faced with a reason to dissuade shoreside bon voyage celebrations because of the high price port authorities charge to clear up the clutter of messy streamers, etc. Many cruise ships leave from ports in the Caribbean. Friends and relatives cannot be expected to fly from Chicago to Puerto Rico just for a bon voyage party.

However, parties during the cruise are still popular and given for all sorts of reasons.It is easy to enjoy yourself at a party on board. And so far, authorities have yet to introduce a Breathalyzer test to see if you are capable of walking back to your cabin.

At this point I am reminded of a joke. It concerns an Irish police officer who was waiting outside a pub in Dublin. The pub had just closed when he saw a man leaving the hostelry and making his unsteady way to the car park. The officer walked over and, taking him by the arm, asked him if he had a car in the car park. The drunk looked at him and, in a voice slurred and slow, said, "Indeed I have, Officer." The officer, looking at him in a disapproving manner said, "And are you going to drive it?" "I most certainly am, Officer," the drunk replied emphatically. "Thank God for that," said the officer, "you're in no fit state to walk."

The reasons for a party on board can vary. Problematic and accidental circumstances have initiated some of the best parties I have ever attended. I remember one very good party on the aft deck when we had been delayed because the propeller had fallen off. Another when we lost our anchor in Grand Cayman (they never did find it). However, there was one special party, given by a passenger, which I and many others will always remember. It was held for a reason that I hope will not happen again.

It never ceases to amaze me in these technically advanced days that ships' architects and builders still make unbelievable mistakes. By now, one would have thought they would be aware of the pitfalls in the design and operation of a cruise ship. Well, they aren't! Last week I was told of four major errors on a new cruise ship, one of them costing a quarter of a million dollars to rectify.

In 1981 the *Royal Viking Star* was "stretched" by nearly ninety feet: the ship was cut in half and the new section floated in. I flew to Bremerhaven to organize my area and get the staff and artists rehearsed for special shows. We sailed across the Atlantic to Fort Lauderdale, where we were to board seven hundred passengers for our maiden voyage. The cruise would take us into the Caribbean, through the Panama Canal to the Mexican Riviera, and from there to our home port, San Francisco.

The new *Star* had nine penthouse suites situated on the sun deck, each costing eight hundred dollars per person per day; they were the most expensive accommodations on the ship. These superdeluxe suites came with a bar, a private verandah, a butler, and a maid. Every day (at the company's expense) the bar was replenished to ensure that the "premier" passenger never got thirsty.

It was just after most of our passengers and guests had boarded, that I heard our chairman, Mr. Warren Titus, being paged on the public-address system. Normally, we try to locate senior executives before paging them, so I realized it had to be something urgent. At the time of the announcement, I was leaving my cabin for a bon voyage party in penthouse two. Passing penthouse eight, I looked in through the open door and saw Mr. Titus. The occupant was telling him, in no uncertain terms, what he thought of his penthouse. My curiosity got the better of me, so I stopped and listened. The passenger was saying, "If you think I am going to pay this amount of money for a penthouse with a tender in front of my verandah, you must be crazy. I want one with a view."

Mr. Titus was his usual calm and sympathetic self, explaining to the passenger that all the other penthouse suites were taken, but he would see if any other suites were available. At that point I left for my party, wondering if I was going to be faced with the same situation. Fortunately, it turned out to be a problem exclusive to penthouse eight.

A few days into the cruise, I received an invitation to a tender party in penthouse eight. By now most of the ship had heard about the "room with no view." The invitation requested guests be there at 6:00 P.M. I arrived at 6:30 to a packed suite and a tender festooned with balloons and streamers. This was against the rules, but it was diplomatically overlooked by the captain.

As soon as I put my foot in the door, the butler handed me a glass of Dom Perignon, and the stewardess a plate of caviar and smoked salmon. It was fairly obvious this was going to be one heck of a party, and expensive too. The butler was continually bringing in enough champagne to float a tender. Nobody seemed interested in going to dinner. This was compensated for by bringing dinner to the suite.

The chef arrived with a huge turkey, which he started to carve. This was followed by a continual flow of more food. The dining room was depleted, as was the show, casino, and nightclub; it would seem that the whole ship had been invited. The party continued through the night, and by dawn some twenty guests remained. Those who had made it through the night were rewarded with a breakfast of bacon and eggs, plus champagne, served in the tender.

The butler told me later, that eighty-nine bottles of Dom Perignon had been polished off as well as three kilos of caviar. At a rough estimate, for those two items alone, it had cost our generous host nine thousand dollars! I could not believe he had taken the situation in such good humor and been so generous. However, none of us knew at the time, that Mr. Titus had given him a generous refund for the loss of his view.

A few days later, a periscope was delivered to penthouse eight as a gift from the staff. The card thanked him for the fabulous party and hoped the periscope would allow him to "see the sea."

The beautiful romantic views of the moon spreading its rays across the nighttime waters would never be seen by any occupant in penthouse eight. The only advantage they would have would be to walk straight into their own tender in case of an emergency. The davit, on which the tender was hung, was too low. I understand this situation has now been rectified.

There is a sequel to this story. The next occupant of penthouse eight, on our cruise back to Fort Lauderdale, never mentioned a word about the tender blocking his view. Apparently, according to the butler, he had a fear of open spaces and never walked out on the verandah. A pity, because we were all looking forward to another party.

Food Glorious Food

I am often asked what are the ingredients of a good cruise and in what order. Well, here is my recipe. Take a well-built and well-designed ship. Keep it spanking clean. Fill it with a happy, caring crew, giving excellent service. Present, with style, a great variety of well-prepared and tasty food. Offer wholesome, family entertainment with a full, varied daily program. All you need after that is to stir in a lot of sunshine.

I know some cruise directors think differently and consider food number one, but it really depends on the clientele. Ships charging high daily rates can afford to present more exotic and expensive foods. However, in my experience, many other lines produce very good fare. Regency Cruises, especially, has an excellent rating. A ship feeds and waters its passengers every two hours, and the more variety you give your guests, the better they like it. A beautifully presented ethnic buffet is always a favorite.

On a Royal Viking ship, the passengers and crew look forward to Norwegian Day. It begins at lunchtime with the most magnificent buffet you will ever see set up in the main lounge bedecked with Norwegian flags. The presentation is a masterpiece of the culinary art. Long tables are decorated with ice carvings, butter sculptures, and food related to the host country displayed in the most appetizing way. The dessert table extends over the width of the lounge. It is a breathtaking display of the pastry chef's skills. The chefs and the assistant chefs are presented by the captain, who makes an appreciative speech before he officially opens the buffet. Throughout the meal, the orchestra plays Norwegian music, adding a special flavor to the feast. The Scandinavians really know how to put on a show when it comes to food.

In the evening you enjoy the second event of the day, a formal Norwegian dinner. This includes, among other things, delicious Norwegian salmon and reindeer meat. The meal is accompanied by the famous Norwegian drink, aquavit. This is made from the Norwegian grape, known to the rest of the world as the potato. Royal Viking Line has its own brand and carries it in old brandy casks in the forward hold, where it matures as the ship crosses the equator and sails around the world. After a year or so, it is landed back in Norway and bottled especially for their passengers.

Aquavit is a drink that must be treated with utmost respect. The tradition is to drink it down in one go and follow it with a glass of Norwegian beer. This, surprising enough, is supposed to tone down its effects. It is unwise to drink it in any quantity. Two small shot glasses are quite sufficient for the average drinker and only one for the casual imbiber. It is the most potent drink I have ever come across and can lure the boastful drinker into a world not previously visited.

It was 1975, and I was enjoying my very first Norwegian Day dinner. Senior officers and staff, who host tables in the dining room, were given a bottle encased in ice for their guests. I was pleased to see that the hotel manager had put a bottle of aquavit on our table. I have been fortunate to have what is known in drinking circles as "hollow legs." I originally came from a long line of teetotalers with strong constitutions. I drank my first beer at twenty-two years of age, and in doing so lost an inheritance from my strict T. T. godfather. The stamp collection he had promised me, would today have been worth well over half a million pounds. That small beer I imbibed was the most expensive drink ever drunk. However, since that time, after enjoying many different beverages, aquavit held no fears for me.

My Norwegian dinner table consisted of seven hard-drinking passengers. Previous nights had proved that, with martinis to start plus two or three bottles of wine and liqueurs to complete the meal. I was told, as the new boy on the block, to make sure the passengers were made aware of the high alcoholic content of the potato spirit. It was a futile effort. My dinner table guests knocked off the first bottle after the appetizer, plus a few beers. Two other bottles followed and the effects of it started to show. Their speech became slurred, their appetites waned, and a general disorientation took place. In the end, only one of them could rise from the table; the others had lost most of their known senses and the use of their legs, the most embarrassing and unfortunate effects of the drink. There was no difficulty in keeping them at the table. I did not want the other passengers to see their predicament, so I waited for the rest of the dining room to clear. No way would they leave without assistance.

Unfortunately, I was not the only one with this problem. The chief engineer had his hands full also. One of his guests was suffering from another "side effect" of the aquavit, i.e., hysteria. A well-dressed and previously elegant, reserved passenger was now, for no apparent reason, screaming with uncontrollable laughter. His body rocked back and forth until suddenly he slipped off his chair and disappeared under the table. The chief and the man's wife were doing their best to get him out but to no avail. He seemed to like it under there.

Eventually, two waiters managed to get hold of his feet; unfortunately, the only appendages available. It was the first time I had seen a passenger dragged out from under a table in that manner or in any other, come to that. Eventually, they got him on his feet but not for long. He sank once again to the floor and tried to make his way back under the table. All this activity was accompanied by his hysterical laughter. The waiters got him half-way up on his knees again and, in that dragged him out of the dining room laughing his head off.

Meanwhile, at my table, I had to get the assistance of the waiters to literally carry out two of my guests and help the others back to their cabins. All this time screams of laughter was still heard from the foyer as others tried to get our hysterical friend in the elevator and down to the hospital. Perhaps the most embarrassing thing for his wife was that on the previous day this seemingly conservative gent had given a talk in the cinema on corporate business. He happened to be the chairman of a most prestigious company. Fortunately, not many of his shareholders witnessed his outrageous predicament, and no drop in his company's shares was reported.

The Norwegian Dancers and Folkloric Show followed the dinner, and I was there as host. The entertainers were mostly made up of the Norwegian crew and were attired in their national costume. This show was one of the highlights of any RVL cruise and always received (by those who were still capable of doing it) a well-deserved standing ovation.

Whilst watching the performance, I had a couple of aquavits before going upstairs to present the nightclub entertainment. I always made sure that a strong act followed the Norwegian show. My guest artist that night was a man who was to become one of my dearest friends, Larry Adler.

The audience was in a great mood as I walked on the stage to introduce my star performer. "Ladies and gentlemen, tonight we are proud to present one of the world's leading harmonica virtuosos, a man who holds a world of music in his hands, Mr. Larry Adler." With that my once hollow legs gave way under me, and I fell to the floor. Luckily, the audience thought it was a great piece of slapstick and part of the act. I got up as if nothing had happened and made some remark about my legs always going funny when I introduced Larry Adler.

I walked off the stage feeling OK but having no idea why this had happened. I was perfectly sober, my speech was clear, and I wasn't dizzy. I went to the back of the room and stood by the bar. I was very concerned about what had happened. I saw Hugh, my assistant, coming toward me. He smiled and said, "That was a funny bit you did. You must keep that in." I was just going to tell him it was far from funny, when the barman handed me a beer. As I took it from his hand, the beer and I disappeared from his view. I had dropped again like a stone to the floor. Hugh helped me up and realized that I was not doing this for laughs. I was getting worried and asked him to thank Larry and close the show as it would be in my best interest to retire.

I made it to my room and went straight to bed. I was now to experience another curse of aquavit, nightmares. They were horrendous and included being pushed out of an aircraft, murdered by strangulation, and last, drowning. It was at this point I woke up bathed in sweat. Eventually, morning came and with it a mammoth hangover. I had learned my lesson, along with some of the other passengers, to have a healthy respect for the Viking's favorite beverage and the potato from whence it comes.

Many comedians entertaining on board include some

material about the consumption of food. My favorite story is about a passenger who went to the early risers' coffee, then to the breakfast buffet, and from there to the regular-seating breakfast in the dining room. He was next seen in the terrace with a large plate of crackers to go with his three cups of bouillon. At twelve o'clock, he was first in line for the midday lunch buffet. He left there after an hour, just in time to make lunch in the dining room. Teatime saw him with a loaded plate of pastries and tea sandwiches. For happy hour he was well into the hot and cold hors d'oeuvres. At dinner he took two of every course and was again first in line at the midnight buffet, after which he took his tray to a table to start on his sixth full meal of the day. Next to him on the floor there was a white coat. "Oh, my God!" exclaimed a passenger, who had been watching his odyssey, "He's eaten the bus boy."

On long cruises, I always host a table. I do not change tables; I dine with the same passengers, be it for fourteen days or one hundred. I consider the dining table the most important social event of the day. If you have a good table, nine times out of ten you will have a good cruise. The larger the table, the more fun and interest is generated; not only that, but sometimes a lot of weight as a by-product. At one of my world cruise tables, eight passengers accumulated some 110 pounds in the ninety days.

You can't always please everybody regarding food. I remember one couple who sent practically everything back to the kitchen. The food was either too cold, not cooked enough, or not what they ordered. They seemed to be the only dissatisfied passengers in the dining room. Their constant loud behavior got on everybody's nerves. However, they were noticed and received a lot of attention, which is usually the intention of people of this sort. There was just no pleasing them. If they had ordered frogs' legs that were not in the kneeling position, they would have sent them back.

The passengers, let alone the waiters, were getting fed up with their incessantly loud complaining. After the maître d' had done everything he could, he asked the hotel manager to deal with the situation personally. The hotel manager couldn't get anywhere with the couple either and things finally got to the point where he told them they would either have to eat in their cabin or leave the ship. Fortunately for all, they decided to leave the ship. The news got around, and the next night, after they had left their table, the band played "Auld Lang Syne" at their empty table to the amusement and applause of the passengers.

It is rare for a good waiter to show his feelings, but there are times when a waiter has to put up with an awful lot. One evening this particular waiter was serving a very difficult man. The waiter had bent over backwards to please him but to no avail. At the end of the twenty-eight day cruise the waiter received no envelope containing recompense for his untiring efforts. Gratuities are usually given on the last evening or at the last breakfast. It happened at neither. A waiter is not allowed to solicit gratuities, but after breakfast, he decided to go down to the passenger's cabin. The man answered the door, and the waiter asked if by chance he had forgotten the service fee. The man made it clear that he would give nothing and pushed the waiter out of the cabin. Push became shove and a fight ensued—the outcome being, the passenger left the ship in an ambulance and the waiter was arrested.

On one long South Seas' cruise, Barbara had a very difficult table. Most of her mealtimes were spent trying to keep a conversation going. Her guests had little in common, save the fact they had all been reassigned from other tables that did not want their company. On top of that, none of them liked each other. This particular evening, however, was obviously going to be worse than most. Two of the rejects had walked off separately after an argument. The rest found nothing right with the food, three of them sending back the entree for one reason or another. Barbara was doing her best to keep the subject off food and more on the next port.

It was time for birthday celebrations and Barbara left to accompany the band and the waiters to the various tables of those enjoying a birthday or some other anniversary. They had just left the first celebratory table, when she and the rest of the passengers heard the sound of breaking glass and china. She looked in the direction of the commotion to see her waiter jumping around on top of her table, the china and glasses being smashed to pieces as he danced around like a whirling dervish.

The headwaiters pulled him down as Barbara and the maître d' escorted her terrified passengers out of the dining room and into the lounge, where she bought them all a large brandy. The straw that had broken the camel's back was having to take a steak back for the third time. The next day, with a new waiter at the table, Barbara no longer had to make polite conversation; they all had plenty to talk about.

People say to me "Oh, it must be wonderful to have caviar whenever you want it and to eat like a king every day." To tell you the truth, no matter how good it is, you become weary of the finest cuisine. As Gilbert said, "When every blessed thing you hold is made of silver or of gold, you long for simple pewter."

It was the last night of the world cruise and the captain's farewell dinner was being served. The usual menu consists of beluga caviar, Maine lobster, beef Wellington, and baked Alaska. When the waiter came to ask for my order, I looked up and, to the surprise of both him and those of my table, said, "Would you kindly ask the chef if he could cook me some bacon and eggs?" And so he did. The only addition was a little black caviar sprinkled on top of the eggs. It was, after all, the captain's farewell dinner.

My wife and I sailed for four years with Royal Viking on their Oriental cruises. On our cruises to China the passengers would disembark for three days to visit Beijing and the Great Wall. On one visit, after disembarking our passengers, the *Royal Viking Star* anchored eighteen miles out. The harbor master needed our docking space for one of the many ships waiting out in the channel to unload. Only passengers who were not well stayed on board. This rarely numbered more than half a dozen at most. The captain would allow the crew to enjoy some of the passenger areas at this time, and the Welfare Committee and myself organized several events to keep the crew happy and occupied. There were all the usual things, i.e., crew concert, horse racing, jackpot bingo, and so forth. However, the best thing we ever had was an international cooking contest. One must remember that most of the waiters, cooks, etc., had been to hotel schools, and we had over thirty nationalities on board.

The dining room that seated over seven hundred passengers was stripped. French cafés, Italian restaurants, Portuguese fishing villages, Philippine beach cafés were built. It was remarkable. One of my most prized photographs is of Barbara's hot Polish pigeon stand in honor of the Polish band. The passengers left on board and the captain were the judges. When the passengers returned from Beijing and heard about the evening, many wished they had stayed.

A large American meat company would send a container of fresh meat out to RVL ships no matter where we were.The port agent would be responsible for having it brought to the ship from the airport. On one occasion, we were sailing out of Sydney, Australia. Head office informed us that a container would be waiting for us on our next call. On arrival the agent told us that no container had been received. We called our head office in San Francisco, which in turn contacted the airline. They said it had been flown out on the previous day. Another search ensued, both at the dock and at the airport; there was no trace of the container. We informed the head office but finally sailed that evening without it. Later that night we had a telex from San Francisco telling us the container had been found . . . in Sydney, Nova Scotia!

When RVL first set sail, the complement of waiters were mostly recruited from five-star hotels in Europe. Our cuisine was mainly European. Many of the waiters had never been to the States and few had served Americans as a group. American table manners are different from those of Europeans, and some of the utensils we had were not familiar to our guests—fish knives, escargot tongs, and finger bowls, for example. On one occasion, in the early days of the line, a passenger at my table complained about the slow service; I had to admit that this was so. I turned to the service area and beckoned to the waiter. "They are complaining about the service being slow," I said quietly in his ear. "They haven't finished yet, sir," he replied. The passenger who had pointed out the situation said abruptly, "We have finished, young man."

The waiter then took the plates away. Later, as I left the table, he accompanied me to the exit. "I'm sorry about that, sir, but they had not put their knives and forks together. I assumed, as most of them still had food on their plates that they had not finished." Aside from the knife and fork ritual to signal that one is finished, it is customary to tidy up one's plate, by pushing food neatly to the side of the plate, not to leave it looking like a battlefield.

The wine waiters also came in for a bit of stick. The American habit of drinking coffee at the start of the meal and then asking for a fine wine to chase it down was repulsive to some of the purists, and the waiters would not pour the wine when a passenger was drinking coffee.

These, of course, were growing pains and the meetings held by the maître d' before the meals, which are held to acquaint the waiters with the menu, quickly cleared up these points.

Chinese food has always been a favorite of ours, so when we started to cruise China and the Orient, we enjoyed many wonderful meals, some more memorable than others. Dining out in a province of that vast country can be quite an experience.

As we were coming to the end of our China, Orient season, I decided to take my staff out for a meal. This has become a tradition with me and as we ate rather "posh" on the ship, I went for the more off-beat venue. This time I decided we would have a special Chinese dinner. What better place to have it than the Seaman's Club in the port of Zincheng.

There were twenty-five of us who left the ship that evening to visit an establishment where the dress code was always very casual. My invitations requested formal attire. The Seaman's Club had never seen a more strangely attired group of people. I had arranged for a table to seat all of us. It was at the end of the very long dining room, where large Oriental screens had been placed to give us some privacy and, I think, also to save the rest of the clientele any embarrassment. We spared ourselves nothing. The food kept coming and coming and the wine and beer flowed. I have never seen so many of my staff four sheets to the wind.

As it was getting late, I called for the bill. The rest of the room was empty and in darkness. The waiter collected his money and, in leaving, pulled back the large screen. I noticed some movement on the floor in the other part of the empty dining room. On closer inspection, I saw to my horror that the floor was covered with rats! The Chinese have the delightful habit of spitting out food on the floor, and these critters were the clean-up crew. I slowly turned to my assistant, and quietly told him to take a look to his right. He leapt up and screamed at the top of his voice, "RATS." Apparently he had a phobia about them. You have never seen people sober up so quickly. The screams from the women scattered the rats in every direction. There was a mad rush for the doors leading out of the dining room.

I do not share the same fear of rats, so my departure was somewhat more dignified and stately. I briskly followed my gang into the corridor leading to the main entrance. All of a sudden the tide turned, and the crew started running back toward me. A large rat was taking its constitutional down the hallway ahead of them. However, it decided to disappear through a door rather than make its way through my team. As they turned again to leave, nature called me to visit the gents' room.

I entered the dirtiest restroom I could ever wish to see. Nature's call was not satisfied as staring at me from in the urinal was the brother of the rat we had just avoided, but this one was bigger. I left at great speed, eager to inform the others of my experience, but they had long since left the scene. The word "ratified" had taken on a new meaning for all of us.

Passengers are always impressed by the pastry cooks on cruise ships. The magnificent desserts and pastries are always a number-one feature. On RVL, the pastry cooks had a great reputation when it came to special cakes. They would bake whatever concoction any passenger requested. The one they baked for my wedding was so big, we could not get it through the doorway of the suite. Cakes are made for many different occasions, but the chef had never one for the event I had in mind. It required a large black chocolate cake suitably inscribed.

Naturally with some five hundred people on board there are bound to be many birthdays and anniversaries, all of them celebrated by the staff, musicians, and their waiters. The cake is rolled in with the assembled company singing the appropriate song.

It was on a sixty-seven-day Circle Pacific cruise when I found, to my surprise, that none of the passengers at my table were celebrating a birthday or an anniversary. We were all rather disappointed. As I left the table I was racking my brains to think what on earth we could celebrate. The answer came to me the next day. In six days' time I would have been divorced from my first wife for one year. Nobody to my knowledge had ever celebrated a divorce day before, so why not next week?

The evening before the celebration, I told my table there was to be a special event celebrated the next night. They were all rather surprised after what had been declared previously. I arranged with all who were to be part of the celebratory preparations what I needed for this "very special" occasion. They all promised to keep it a secret.

The next evening the passengers were a little non-plussed when all the waiters were wearing black armbands. They told the passengers that all would be revealed later. After the desserts had been served, the lights went down. The sound of the band playing the death march from "Saul" came from the back of the dining room. Behind them came the "padre" and my staff, all wearing black. The ladies were wearing veils and sobbing beneath them. The waiters marched in from the other end of the dining room led by the maître d' carrying the large black chocolate cake. They arrived at the table to hoots of laughter and to some bemused looks from the other passengers. The cake was placed in front of me, on it inscribed, "Happy Divorce Day, Uncle Derek."

The band stopped playing and the padre read a short eulogy of my marriage in rhyme. At the end of it, the band struck up, and the staff and waiters sang "Happy Divorce Day," in a minor key however. The cake was cut, and after that production, passengers came up and wished me, yes, you've guessed it, "Happy birthday, Derek."

Down to the Seas Again

I trust I have not yet come to the end of my travels, but I have come to the conclusion of this book. There are many more stories I would like to relate, but they will have to be written some other time.

Time and again we have so often thought of leaving the ships and the sea. Coming back after a long contract to our home on Cape Cod, taking our boat out into Buzzards Bay, playing golf, and enjoying the beach, we often ask ourselves, "Why do we always go back?"

But in my study, I look out to the ocean, and as a cruise ship starts to make its way into the Cape Cod Canal, I sigh and say, "Come on, Barbara, it's that time again. The sea has called us back once more."

Little can compare with sailing on a beautiful cruise ship out of a tropical island, set in a clear, blue sky. As the ship makes its way out of the harbor, the lush green mountains start to change color as the evening light loses its brilliance.

The wake of the ship laps the harbor wall and caresses the beach beyond. Soon, it is clear of the buoys that mark the safe exit, and the ship, with only half an hour before sunset, glides its way out into the strait and toward the continuing chain of islands. Their unique mountains soar up into the clouds, hanging over them like a mantle. The sky constantly changes color and shape, as clouds roll upwards, touched by the cooler air of evening. As they rise and roll, the sun starts its descent behind them. Its rays suddenly explode into a hundred shafts of light. From behind the white mass of clouds, the sky starts to glow a fiery red. Then, at the last dying moments of the sun's daily life, an opening appears below the streaks of pink cloud. The sun lays itself upon its horizon bed and sinks into its nightly slumber. All too soon, it is gone, and the miracle of another sunset has passed away, a fitting close to a magical day in some tropical island paradise or some magnificently unspoiled Arctic landscape.

The air starts to chill as the ship changes course and heads into the increasing wind, filling the void made by the rising warmer air. It catches your hair, and the sound of the sea rushing against the hull increases in volume as the ship starts to make more speed toward its next rapturous port.

The magic of the ships and the sea has just seduced another lover, and between them, they have cast their spell. Recalling them, you will always be reminded of that romantic and unforgettable moment when your first ship sailed into the sunset, and you became a slave of a demanding, but enchanting, mistress, a cruise ship. Who would ever consider experiencing a vacation in any other way?

IV

Cruising Tips

Before the cruise

Make sure you have:
- Tickets, money, and, if needed, your passport with visas where required (check this with your travel agent or cruise line).
  Note: Do *not* put them in your luggage!
- Regarding money: Allow for the cost of local transportation and tipping of porters at airport and ship. One dollar a bag is an acceptable rate.
  Regarding money for tipping at the end of the cruise: Allow approximately $9.00 a day. Service staff rarely have bank accounts and, on some ships, personal checks are not accepted and cash is not given for credit cards. Take either cash, or, preferably, traveler's checks.
- Camera, film and binoculars
  Make sure to pack:
- Prescription medication, Dramamine, Maalox, etc.
- *Very important.* Do not put important medication in your luggage. Keep important pills on your person or in your hand luggage.
- Your telephone and address book
- Toilet bag
- A good book to read
  Attach *two* labels securely to your baggage:
- One is the shipping-line label showing your port of embarkation, your cabin number, etc. This tag should be taken off on the last day of the voyage when the disembarkation color or numbered tag is put on.
  The other is your personal tag that should be permanently on your bag with your name, street address (not P.O. Box) and telephone number.
  Note: Barbara's tip: With so many bags looking alike,

festoon each bag with colored ribbons for easy identification at luggage claim.

Check that you have:

- Closed all the windows
- Locked all the doors
- Set time switches for security lights
- Turned off the oven
- Provided for the animals
- Taken your house keys
- Taken care of the mail

On the cruise

- Don't expect your baggage to be in your room on
arrival. There could be some 2,000 bags to be delivered.
- The first night, be tolerant and patient with your table
mates—it usually pays off in the end.
- Do not overeat—you might pay later.
- Keep fit. Walk the decks as much as possible and try
not to use the elevators unless you have a physical
problem.
- Review the daily program every night for the next
day's schedule of events and important announcements from the Purser's office.

If you are taking a tour:

- Check the daily program for the tour's departure
time from the ship or the shore.
- Make sure you know the time of sailing and, if ten-
dering, the time of the last boat leaving from the shore
to the ship.
- Remember, if you miss the ship, you are financially

responsible for getting back to it at the next port of call.

- Ship life is different. Do not fester with a situation or problem that gets under your skin. See the Purser's office or the cruise director. You are on a cruise to enjoy yourself.
- Do not leave all your packing until the last night of the cruise. Pack things away when you have finished with them.

Last day of the cruise

- When finishing packing, make sure you leave something out to wear for the next day!
- Attend the "Disembarkation" talk for information regarding leaving the ship and for Immigration and Customs formalities.
- Settle any gratuities that evening. This will ensure that the service staff gets a good night's sleep.
- So that you can keep in touch with newfound friends, take your address book and some calling cards down to dinner.

Disembarkation Day

- Make sure you look under the bed and check drawers and cupboards. Look behind the bathroom door.
- Leave your room keys on the cabin dresser.
- Assemble in the public lounges for announcements. On no account stand in foyers or gangway areas or sit on staircases.

- When finally leaving the baggage hall, have your customs form ready at hand for the Customs officials.
- Have a safe journey home.